Two Men, Two Acts, Two Results

– – The Gospel According To Paul – –

By

J. A. YOUNGBERG

Bible Teacher

Foreword by

J. OLIVER BUSWELL, JR.

WIPF & STOCK · Eugene, Oregon

FOREWORD

I am happy to call to the attention of my friends this stimulating and thoughtful study in the fifth chapter of the Epistle to the Romans. Our Brother Youngberg has a deep appreciation of the hopelessly lost condition of man in his natural state, and of the marvelous work of Christ, Who saves His people by grace alone.

The reader will doubtless disagree with Brother Youngberg in certain points. I must confess that the press of duties has prevented me from giving this work the prolonged study which it merits. However, I can testify in all earnestness that every reader will receive a great blessing from the pages.

J. OLIVER BUSWELL, JR.

Wipf and Stock Publishers
199 W 8th Ave, Suite 3
Eugene, OR 97401

Two Men, Two Acts, Two Results
The Gospel According to Paul
By Youngberg, J. A. and Buswell, J. Oliver, Jr.
ISBN 13: 978-1-61097-163-8
Publication date 12/21/2010
Previously published by Fundamental Truth Publishers, 1939

PREFACE

Many years ago I heard the late Dr. James M. Gray say, "Consecutive gospel preaching will result in the salvation of souls." This book is an attempt to so present the Gospel of Grace. The substance of it has for the past several years been taught in Bible Conferences and Classes.

The Lord has blessed it to the salvation of precious souls. Many Christians have been stripped of legal bondage and entered into the glorious liberty that only the Grace of God can give. Many of these have asked for the material in some permanent form. All I have had to offer was a copy of the chart.

During the past several months I have taught the series in a Bible Class at the local Y. W. C. A. Most excellent notes have been taken by Miss Marien Kindberg, "my true child in the faith." Together we have prepared the contents of this book.

We have endeavored to let the Word speak for itself, and not present our own opinions.

The Purpose of this book is to set forth the Gospel of Grace—the good news concerning Christ and Him crucified—and that alone. It is sent forth with the prayer that through the reading of these pages many will be led out of darkness into the glorious light of God's Love, and that the Lord's people will be further equipped to render unto Him effectual service, having a more thorough working knowledge of the Gospel of Grace, so important in true Christian testimony—all in all that our blessed Redeemer and Lord may be glorified!

J. A. YOUNGBERG.

Jamestown, N. Y.
June 1, 1939.

CONTENTS

	PAGE
INTRODUCTION	7

SECTION ONE: ADAM—THE FIRST MAN

CHAPTER I—THE ONE ACT OF DISOBEDIENCE — 13
Adam's Original State; Adam's Responsibility; Adam's Temptation and Fall.

CHAPTER II—THE RESULT OF ADAM'S ORIGINAL SIN UPON ADAM AND EVE — 21
They Became Involved in the Sentence of Death; Their Eyes Were Opened; They Became Sinners; They Acquired Guilt; They Were Summoned into God's Presence; They Were Expelled from the Garden; Their Authority over Creation Was Lost.

CHAPTER III—THE RESULT OF ADAM'S ORIGINAL SIN UPON THE RACE — 25
Man Became a Sinner by Imputation; Man Became a Sinner in Nature; Man Became a Sinner in Action; Man Is Now a Sinner by a Judicial Reckoning.

CHAPTER IV—THE RESULT OF GOD'S JUDGMENT UPON ADAM'S ORIGINAL SIN — 39
Total Depravity; Enslavement to Sin and to Satan; A Blinded Mind; Corrupted Affections; Death—The Penalty of Sin; Creation Subjected to Vanity.

SECTION TWO: THE LAW

CHAPTER V—THE LAW — 51
Conditions Before the Law; The Nature of the Law.

CHAPTER VI—WHAT THE LAW COULD NOT DO — 57
Prescribed Duty—Provided No Motive; Demanded Obedience—Could Not Make Obedient; Required Righteousness—Could Not Make Righteous; Revealed Sin—Could Not Remove Sin; Enslaved—Could Not Set Free; Condemned to Death—Could Not Give Life; Made Nothing Perfect.

CHAPTER VII—"WHEREFORE THEN SERVETH THE LAW?" 63
To Give the Knowledge of Sin; To Stop Every Mouth; To Bring Under Judgment to God; To Give to Sin the Character of Transgression; To Curse and Condemn; To Minister Death; To Lead to Christ.

SECTION THREE: CHRIST—THE SECOND MAN

CHAPTER VIII—THE INCARNATION - - - 71
  Biblical Reasons for the Incarnation—To Reveal God; To Reveal Man; To Provide a Mediator; To Provide the Sacrifice for Sin; To Provide a Merciful and Faithful High Priest; To Destroy the Works of the Devil; To Fulfill the Davidic Covenant; To Provide the Head of the Church.

CHAPTER IX—THE VIRGIN BIRTH - - - 81
  Reasons for the Necessity of the Virgin Birth—That Prophecy Might Be Fulfilled; That Christ Might Be Entitled to the Throne of David; That Sinners Might Have a Saviour.

CHAPTER X—THE ONE ACT OF OBEDIENCE - 87
  Things Accomplished by Christ's Death on the Cross—Imputed Sin Dealt With; Sin in Nature Dealt With; Sin in Action Dealt With; Pre-Cross Sins Dealt With; Satan Judged; Law Ended; Redemption Accomplished; Reconciliation Accomplished; Propitiation Made; The Ground of Justification Accomplished; Peace Made; The Means of Perpetual Cleansing Provided; The Sting of Death Removed; A New and Living Way Consecrated; The New Covenant Confirmed; The Covenant of Redemption Confirmed; Those Who Were Afar Off Made Nigh; The Blessing of Abraham Released; The Way Opened for God To Exercise Both Justice and Mercy; The Sanctified Forever Perfected.

CHAPTER XI—CHRIST'S BURIAL AND RESURRECTION 119
  "He Was Buried"; "He Rose Again"; Biblical Reasons for the Resurrection—Because He Was the Son of God; To Fulfill Prophecy; Because the Ground of Justification Was Accomplished; To Bestow Resurrection Life; To Impart Resurrection Power; To Be the Head over All Things to the Church; To Be the Firstfruits and the Pattern.

CHAPTER XII—THE ASCENSION AND SESSION OF CHRIST 129
  The Two Ascensions; Christ's Present Ministry—He Is Bestowing Gifts to the Church; He Is Interceding for His Own; He Is Advocating for His Own; He Is Preparing a Place for His Own

SECTION FOUR: THE RESULT OF THE ONE ACT OF OBEDIENCE

CHAPTER XIII—THE NEW CREATION IN CHRIST JESUS 139
CHAPTER XIV—SERVICE AND REWARDS - - 149

INTRODUCTION
TWO MEN, TWO ACTS, AND TWO RESULTS

I Cor. 15:45-50; Rom. 5:12-21.

And so it is written, The first man Adam was made a living soul; the last Adam was made a quickening spirit.

Howbeit that was not first which was spiritual, but that which is natural; and afterward that which is spiritual.

The first man was of the earth, earthy: the second man is the Lord from heaven.

As is the earthy, such are they also that are earthy: and as is the heavenly, such are they also that are heavenly.

And as we have borne the image of the earthy, we shall also bear the image of the heavenly.

Now this I say, brethren, that flesh and blood cannot inherit the kingdom of God; neither doth corruption inherit incorruption.

Wherefore, as by one man sin entered into the world, and death by sin; and so death passed upon all men, for that all have sinned:

For until the law sin was in the world: but sin is not imputed when there is no law.

Nevertheless death reigned from Adam to Moses, even over them that had not sinned after the similitude of Adam's transgression, who is the figure of him that was to come.

But not as the offence, so also is the free gift. For

if through the offence of the one many be dead, much more the grace of God, and the gift by grace, which is by one man, Jesus Christ, hath abounded unto many.

And not as it was by one that sinned, so is the gift: for the judgment was by one to condemnation, but the free gift is from many offences unto justification.

For if by one man's offence death reigned by one; much more they which receive abundance of grace and of the gift of righteousness shall reign in life by one Jesus Christ.

Therefore as by the offence of one judgment came upon all men to condemnation; even so by the righteousness of one the free gift came upon all men unto justification of life.

For as by one man's disobedience many were made sinners, so by the obedience of one shall many be made righteous.

Moreover the law entered, that the offence might abound. But where sin abounded, grace did much more abound:

That as sin hath reigned unto death, even so might grace reign through righteousness unto eternal life by Jesus Christ our Lord.

These two extended passages of New Testament Scripture form the basis of the message of this book. Two men, Adam and Christ, are clearly in view in both passages. The Apostle Paul contrasts the two in a most logical and convincing way. He brings out the completeness and the far-reaching results of Christ's work by contrasting it with the work of Adam.

Briefly stated, the two men are Adam and Christ; the two acts, Adam's disobedience (Gen. 3:6) and Christ's obedience (Phil. 2:8); the two results, condemnation and justification (Rom. 5:18).

Adam was a type of Christ, in that he was a representative man; he stood for the race, he contained the race, he was the race. He was without a parallel until Christ, the Second Man, the last Adam, came. He was "the figure of him that was to come."

Note also how the Apostle Paul applies a most important principle stated so many times in the first chapter of Genesis, "after its kind," "after their kind."

SECTION ONE

ADAM—THE FIRST MAN

CHAPTER I.
THE ONE ACT OF DISOBEDIENCE
Adam's Original State

And God said, Let us make man in our image, and after our likeness: and let them have dominion over the fish of the sea, and over the fowl of the air, and over the cattle, and over all the earth, and over every creeping thing that creepeth upon the earth.

So God created man in his own image, in the image of God created he him; male and female created he them.

And God blessed them, and said unto them, Be fruitful, and multiply, and replenish the earth, and subdue it: and have dominion over the fish of the sea, and over the fowl of the air, and over every living thing that moveth upon the earth.

And God saw every thing that he had made, and, behold, it was very good (Gen. 1:26-28, 31).

And the LORD God formed man of the dust of the ground, and breathed into his nostrils the breath of life; and man became a living soul (Gen. 2:7).

The Mosaic record of the creation of man calls to mind the words of the Psalmist, "The heavens, even the heavens are the Lord's; but the earth hath he given to the children of men" (Psalm 115:16).

The creation of man took place on the sixth day, and was undoubtedly delayed until that time in order that the earth might be prepared for his reception.

Man was created unfallen, sinless, and innocent, but not positively holy as was Christ (Luke 1:35), for Adam had the capacity to sin.

As recorded in the Scriptures, man was created in the image of God. This was in the image of Elohim, the creative name of God, and not in the image of Jehovah, His redemptive name. To be like his Redeemer is the hope of the true believer for the future.

Was the image moral, intellectual, or physical?

Since a moral image of God involves a full moral likeness in the divine glories, perfections and attributes of Deity, it cannot be said that man was created in the full moral image of God.

Was the image, then, of full intellectual likeness? No, for although the first man was an intellectual giant, he did not possess the perfect knowledge that he would have had, had he been intellectually like unto God.

This makes it obvious that the image was physical. To this it will be objected that no man can see God and live, and that God is a Spirit. It is true that no man can see God in His essential being and live—but we believe that Christ originally took creature form in order to create, and that it was in the image of Christ, the Creator, that man was created. Note carefully the contents of the following quotations from the Scriptures: "And he said, Hear now my words: If there be a prophet among you, I the LORD will make myself known unto him in a vision, and I will speak unto him in a dream. My servant Moses is not so, who is faithful in all mine house. With him will I speak mouth to mouth, even apparently, and not in dark speeches; and the similitude of the LORD shall he behold: wherefore then were ye not afraid to speak against my servant Moses?" (Numbers 12:6-8); "And unto the angel of the church in Laodicea write: These things saith the Amen, the faithful and true witness, the beginning of the creation of God" (Rev. 3:14); "As for me, I will behold thy face in righteousness: I shall be satisfied, when I awake, with thy likeness" (Psalm 17:15). The Revised Version renders the last word of this verse "form."

In the fall, man lost this form to some extent. The fall affected man spiritually, mentally, morally and physically.

Adam's Responsibility

And God blessed them, and God said unto them, be fruitful, and multiply, and replenish the earth, and subdue it: and have dominion over the fish of the sea, and over the fowl of the air, and over every living thing that moveth upon the earth.

And God said, Behold, I have given you every herb bearing seed, which is upon the face of all the earth, and every tree, in the which is the fruit of a tree yielding seed; to you it shall be for meat (Gen. 1:28, 29).

And the LORD God took the man, and put him into the garden of Eden to dress it and keep it. And the LORD God commanded the man, saying, of every tree of the garden thou mayest freely eat: but of the tree of the knowledge of good and evil, thou shalt not eat of it: for in the day that thou eatest thereof thou shalt surely die (Gen. 2:15-17).

Man was not to spend his time in idleness. Work was prescribed for him. Under the terms of the Edenic covenant, which conditioned the life of man in his unfallen state, he was responsible to do certain things.

To multiply and replenish the restored earth with a new order of beings.

To subdue the earth to human uses.

To have dominion over the rest of creation.

To dress and to keep the garden.

To refrain from eating of the tree of the knowledge of good and evil.

From Genesis 1:29 it is evident that man was to be a vegetarian.

The work prescribed for man was of the easiest kind, and served merely as an agreeable recreation. He was put in the garden of Eden, where nature appeared in all her loveliness—a garden which God Himself had planted, and in which grew "every tree which was pleasant to the sight, and good for food."

In the midst of abundance man experienced no present want, and felt no anxiety with reference to the future; for unconscious of guilt, he looked up with confident expectation to the goodness of his Creator.

Negatively, there was but one restriction imposed upon man in this perfect environment. God strictly forbade him to eat of the tree of the knowledge of good and evil. The penalty for violation of God's commandment was death, "For in the day thou eatest thereof thou shalt surely die." Thus the Edenic covenant was conditional.

Adam's Temptation and Fall

Now the serpent was more subtle than any beast of the field which the LORD God had made. And he said unto the woman, Yea, hath God said, Ye shall not eat of every tree of the garden?

And the woman said unto the serpent, We may eat of the fruit of the trees of the garden:

But of the fruit of the tree which is in the midst of the garden, God hath said, Ye shall not eat of it, neither shall ye touch it, lest ye die.

And the serpent said unto the woman, Ye shall not surely die:

For God doth know that in the day ye eat thereof, then your eyes shall be opened, and ye shall be as gods, knowing good and evil.

And when the woman saw that the tree was good for food, and that it was pleasant to the eyes, and a tree to be desired to make one wise, she took of the fruit thereof, and did eat, and gave also unto her husband with her; and he did eat.

And the eyes of them both were opened, and they knew that they were naked; and they sewed fig leaves together, and made themselves aprons (Gen. 3:1-7).

The Temptation

Since Adam was created upright, and possessed no sin nature, when Satan brought his proposition to him, it was a test rather than a temptation, as we speak of temptations.

No testing is complete apart from three distinct features; neither would Adam's testing have been complete had it not measured up to those requirements.

In order that a testing be fair and just, the real issue must be understood. Since Adam's testing involved the eating of the tree of the knowledge of good and evil, this tree became the issue between God and man. God had instructed Adam concerning this, so that in his testing he was well aware of the issue before him.

Also in a fair testing, he who is tested must possess perfect freedom to act. This point was also included in Adam's testing. Being a free moral agent, he had liberty to do as he pleased, either to obey or to disobey the express commandment of God.

Finally in a just testing there must be the full knowledge of the consequence of failure. God had from the first made it perfectly clear to man that he had full permission to eat of every tree of the garden with the exception of the tree of the knowledge of good and evil, and that in the day he should eat thereof he would surely die (Gen. 2:17).

Satan was permitted to tempt man. "And Adam was not deceived, but the woman being deceived was in the transgression" (I Tim. 2:14).

He tempted him not to anything morally wrong, but it was that man might become an independent being, "Ye shall be as gods knowing good and evil." This calls to mind the words of James, "Then when lust hath conceived, it bringeth forth sin: and sin, when it is finished, bringeth forth death" (James 1:15). That Satan told the truth when he said, "Ye shall be as gods knowing good and evil," is evident from what God said after Adam had sinned, "Behold, the man is become as one of us, knowing good and evil" (Gen. 3:22).

The Fall — The Act of Disobedience

Being upright and free from a sin nature man would not have sinned, and he did not sin apart from the tempter. The words of the tempter were a mixture of truth and lies, such as is always his way of deceiving his victims. When he said, "Ye shall be as gods, knowing good and evil," he spoke the truth, but when he said, "Ye shall not surely die," he lied.

Adam fell from desires which in themselves were not sinful. However, his one act of disobedience involved the repudiation of God and His word, and the exercise of self-will—the very thing that Satan had done, and which had been the cause of his fall. We read, "How art thou fallen from heaven, O Lucifer, son of the morning! how art thou cut down to the ground, which did weaken the nations! For thou hast said in thine heart, I will ascend into heaven, I will exalt my throne above the stars of God: I will sit also upon the mount of the congregation, in the sides of the north: I will ascend above the heights of the clouds; I will be like the most High" (Isa. 14:12-14).

CHAPTER II.

THE RESULT OF ADAM'S ORIGINAL SIN UPON ADAM AND EVE

1. *They Became Involved in the Sentence of Death.*

For in the day that thou eatest thereof thou shalt surely die.

Three aspects of death are revealed in the Scriptures—physical, spiritual, and eternal or the second.

Spiritual death is separation from God. This aspect of death Adam experienced when he ate of the forbidden fruit. Through his sin man lost the favor of God, and became incapable of loving and serving his Creator.

Physical death is the dissolution of the union which obtains between the body and the spirit. Adam did not experience physical death immediately, for he lived on to be nine hundred and thirty years. Though he did not die immediately, his body became mortal. The seeds of mortality were sown in his constitution; a change took place in his body. It was now subject to internal disorders, and external injuries; it was exposed to the wasting influence of the elements. It was doomed to decline in vigor and activity, to feel the infirmities of old age, and at last to sink into the grave—"And he died" (Gen. 5:5).

The second death is the lake of fire, "prepared for the devil and his angels" (Matt. 25:41, Cf. Rev. 20:10,

14, 15). When our Lord says, "And whosoever liveth and believeth in me shall never die" (John 11:26) and "This is the bread which cometh down from heaven, that a man may eat thereof, and not die" (John 6:50), He evidently refers to eternal death, the opposite of eternal life. The believer is not saved from temporal death, for if the Lord tarries death will overtake us, but thank God the sting of death is forever gone for the believer, because Christ on the Cross bore the sting of death (I Cor. 15:55, 56). The second death is not the annihilation of man, but declares him to be in a state of consciousness, because it is a positive punishment. It is what one writer terms "a living death." These "shall have their part in the lake which burneth with fire and brimstone, which is the second death" (Rev. 21:8).

2. *Their Eyes Were Opened,* and they knew they were naked. The fact that their bodies were without a covering they surely knew before; so then, the opening of their eyes and their knowing that they were naked must refer to something more than what is usually considered to be the meaning of the statement.

Instead of acquiring supernatural wisdom, as they had fondly hoped the forbidden fruit would bestow upon them, they discovered that they had reduced themselves to an unprotected and wretched condition. Their original state of sinlessness and innocence was lost, and they were now exposed to the wrath of their Creator.

This may be inferred from Adam's reply to the Lord's question, "Where art thou?" Adam did not say I was ashamed, but "I was afraid because I was naked; and I hid myself."

They were now conscious of guilt, and wished to avoid a meeting with their judge, for such was now

God's relationship to them. Man stood before God as a criminal before a judge. Such is the relationship that obtains between the Lord and every unsaved person.

3. *They Became Sinners.* Through this one act of sin they acquired a sin nature, a disposition to sin, thus becoming sinners. They became sinners because they sinned; the rest of the human family have sinned because they were sinners.

4. *They Acquired Guilt* in that they transgressed the commandment of God. "For until the law sin was in the world: but sin is not imputed (as guilt) when there is no law" (Rom. 5:13); "For where no law is, there is no transgression" (Rom. 4:15).

5. *They Were Summoned into the Presence of God* and sentence was pronounced upon them, by which they were subjected to all the miseries of life, and finally to death. "Dust thou art and unto dust shalt thou return" (Gen. 3:19).

6. *They Were Expelled from Paradise,* which was an abode of the righteous, and not the guilty. "And the LORD God said, Behold, the man is become as one of us, to know good and evil: and now, lest he put forth his hand, and take also of the tree of life, and eat, and live forever; therefore the LORD God sent him forth from the garden of Eden, to till the ground from whence he was taken. So he drove out the man; and he placed at the east of the Garden cherubims, and a flaming sword which turned every way, to keep the way of the tree of life" (Gen. 3:22-24).

7. *The Authority God Had Given to Man over the Rest of Creation (Gen. 1:28) Was Lost* through the Fall, and Satan became "the prince of this world" (John 14:30), as is revealed in the offer of the kingdoms of this world to our Lord in the wilderness temptation (Matt. 4:8-10).

CHAPTER III.

THE RESULT OF ADAM'S ORIGINAL SIN UPON THE WHOLE RACE

Every member of the human family entering the world through natural generation is, through Adam's original sin, constituted a sinner.

Here we must briefly consider what sin is, and get the correct understanding of the sin question. Every heresy can be traced to a wrong conception of sin.

The fall of the human race into a state of sin is the basis and foundation of the scriptural plan of redemption and of all sound gospel preaching and teaching.

"Sin is the trangression of the law" (I John 3:4). "Sin is lawlessness" is the literal rendering of this sentence. This reveals the awful character of sin. It is spiritual anarchy. Sin is any lack of conformity to the infinitely holy and righteous character of God, as revealed in the Law. We read, "All have sinned and come short of the glory of God" (Rom. 3:23).

Here we must distinguish between Adam as the natural head of the race and his federal headship. As the federal head of the race, he was our representative. Therefore, his original act of disobedience may justly be reckoned as ours. This brings us up to the full consideration of the various aspects or classifications of sin.

Imputed Sin

Man is a sinner by imputation. We read, "Wherefore, as through one man sin entered the world, and death by sin; and so death passed upon all men, for that all have sinned" (Rom. 5:12).

According to the original, Paul does not say that "all *have* sinned." It is not true that all have sinned personally. The innocent babe does not die because of any personal sins he has committed. But "all sinned" in Adam, the federal head of the race. Paul uses the Greek aorist tense that expresses a definite act at a definite time in the past.

To impute means to reckon over to. It is expressed in the words of Paul when he says, "If he hath wronged thee, or oweth thee ought, put that on mine account" (Philemon 1:18).

Imputed sin is the primary reason why man is lost. He is born dead in sin, a child of wrath, a son of disobedience (Eph. 2:1-3). He is born into a lost estate, a condemned race. He is therefore lost because of what he is, rather than because of what he does. But remember, he does what he does because of what he is.

Teaching on this aspect of sin has been sadly neglected. Many know nothing about it, and not a few boldly deny the fact of imputed sin. Socinians and Pelagians, and their present day successors, deny that Adam was the federal head of his posterity, and thereby deny the fact of imputed sin. Arminians admit that the whole race was injured by the first sin of the first man, but at the same time refute the proposition that Adam was their proper representative. It is the one aspect of sin that needs to be emphasized again and again.

Many seem to think that while they are not quite

good enough to go to heaven, they most certainly are not bad enough to go to hell. But there is no such person. Man is either good enough to go to heaven, or else bad enough to go to hell. The Bible does not recognize any intermediate ground.

Some years ago a friend asked me to pray for her unsaved relatives, and then she added, "It is impossible to reach them with the Gospel." Was it because they were so bad, that she said this? No, they were so good, humanly speaking, that they could not see that they were lost and in need of a Saviour. Such people need to know the truth under consideration.

But some one asks, "How can it be possible that we sinned in Adam?" Look at the Scripture parallel, "Levi also, who receiveth tithes, paid tithes in Abraham, for he was yet in the loins of his father, when Melchizedek met him" (Heb. 7:9, 10). Levi was the great-grandson of Abraham and was not born until about a hundred and fifty or a hundred and sixty years after the incident referred to in this Scripture. In the same sense, we were in Adam when he sinned, and so we all sinned in him.

The Apostle Paul evidently anticipated objections to what he says in Romans 5:12 "that all sinned," for six times in the remaining verses of the chapter he repeats what he has already declared in verse twelve.

"For if through the offence of one many be dead."

"For the judgment was by one to condemnation."

"For if by one man's offence death reigned by one."

"Therefore as by the offence of one judgment came upon all men to condemnation."

"For as by one man's disobedience many were made sinners."

"That as sin has reigned unto death."

This naturally raises the question of infant salvation. If all of the race are constituted sinners in Adam, how can children who are incapable of believing the Gospel be saved?

Dr. Chas. Hodge, in his commentary on Romans, says on this question, "If without personal participation in the sin of Adam, all men are subject to death, may we not hope that without personal acceptance of the righteousness of Christ, all who die in infancy are saved?"

This question will come before us again, when the finished work of Christ on the Cross will be considered.

Sin In Nature

Man partakes by inheritance of Adam's fallen nature. We read, "And Adam lived an hundred and thirty years, and begat a son in his own likeness, after his image; and called his name Seth" (Gen. 5:3). Paul says, "For as by one man's disobedience many were made sinners, so by the obedience of one shall many be made righteous" (Rom. 5:19). This is a sinful constitution, a disposition to sin. It is a common belief that man becomes a sinner when he commits his first personal sin. This is not absolutely true, for man is a sinner from the moment he is born. David said, "Behold, I was shapen in iniquity; and in sin did my mother conceive me" (Psalm 51:5).

However, he does, at the time that he commits his first personal sin, become a sinner in another aspect— in action.

It is because he is already a sinner by nature that he sins in action. A man lies because he is a liar. He steals because he is a thief. Just so, a man sins because he is a sinner.

Many years ago while doing gospel work in the mountain districts of Southern California, I asked a group of children if it was ever necessary for their parents to tell them to be good. They all answered in the affirmative. Then I asked them if it was necessary for their parents to tell them to be naughty, and the answer was a loud "NO." Then when I asked why this was so, a ten-year-old boy answered, "We are all born crooked." He was right. "The heart is deceitful above all things, and desperately wicked, who can know it?" (Jer. 17:9).

This evil principle we inherit from Adam mediately through our parents, who have themselves received it from the succeeding generations from Adam. It is in the Scriptures called:

The Flesh—"That which is born of the flesh is flesh" (John 3:6). This does not refer to the tissues of the body, but all that the unregenerate man is—body, soul, and spirit.

Concerning the flesh we are definitely told that "the flesh profiteth nothing" (John 6:63). "Because the carnal mind is enmity against God: for it is not subject to the law of God, neither indeed can be. So then they that are in the flesh cannot please God" (Rom. 8:7, 8). "For I know that in me, that is, in my flesh, dwelleth no good thing" (Rom. 7:18).

The Natural Man—This refers to all that are unchanged or dead spiritually. Literally it reads, "the psychical man." The soul is Satan's objective and sphere of activity. Too often psychic manifestations are mistaken for manifestations of the Holy Spirit. "By their fruits ye shall know them."

The natural man may be refined, cultured, kind, a model citizen, sweet, eloquent, and even severely religious, but he "receiveth not the things of the Spirit of God: for they are foolishness unto him: neither can he know them, because they are spiritually discerned" (I Cor. 2:14).

Our Old Man—We read that "he is corrupt according to deceitful lusts" (Eph. 4:22), and that "our old man is (was) crucified with him" (Rom. 6:6).

The Heart—We are told that, "The heart is deceitful above all things, and desperately wicked; who can know it?" (Jer. 17:9). "And God saw that the wickedness of man was great in the earth, and that every imagination of the thoughts of his heart was only evil continually" (Gen. 6:5). "Out of the heart proceed evil thoughts, murders, adulteries, fornications, thefts, false witness, blasphemies" (Matt. 15:19).

Many talk about a change of heart, but this is not scriptural. The old heart (the power to reason) is not changed or made over in salvation. Man is created anew in Christ Jesus when he becomes a Christian.

We have often heard evangelists urge their unsaved hearers to give their hearts to God. As if a lost sinner could do such a thing! And if he could what would God want with the evil thing? No, God is the bestower of a new heart—the divine nature (II Peter 1:4).

The Outward Man—Of him we are told that "he perishes" (II Cor. 4:16). Since the outward man is in this verse placed over against and compared with the inward man, it evidently refers to all that man is in his unregenerate state. It is one of the designations of the sinful nature with which man is burdened as long as he is on earth.

The Carnal Mind—"The carnal mind is enmity against

God; for it is not subject to the law of God, neither indeed can be" (Rom. 8:7).

In Romans 5:10, the unregenerate man is said to be an enemy of God. However, an enemy may be conquered and become the best friend of his conqueror; such is the blessed experience of the saved. But here is something that goes deeper. "The carnal mind is enmity against God"; it has always been so, and it never will be anything else. The sin nature can not be changed. Therefore the old sin nature, that the believer still possesses, is and will ever continue to be just as evil as it was before he was saved, for "that which is born of the flesh is flesh." Thus we see how deep-rooted this evil principle is. It is incurably evil.

Since the old sin nature was crucified with Christ, and is therefore judicially dead, the Holy Spirit is free to come in and take control of it. It is through the indwelling ministry of the Holy Spirit that the believer has the victory over sin. Paul writes, "There is therefore now no condemnation to them that are in Christ Jesus. For the law of the Spirit of life in Christ Jesus hath made me free from the law of sin and death" (Rom. 8:1, 2). For the child of God is provided a means whereby he may have the victory over every enemy.

Sin—We must distinguish between "sin" and "sins." "Sin" is the tree; "sins" are the fruit. In Romans 1:16 to 5:11 it is "sins," the fruit of the sin nature, that are dealt with. The precious blood of Christ is the only cure and remedy for this aspect of sin.

"The wages of sin is death" (Rom. 6:23). Paul does not say "the punishment of sin is death." Too often these two words are considered to be identical.

A man may be hired to commit a crime. He commits it, and he receives his pay for his evil deed; that is his wages. Then he is arrested, tried, convicted of his crime, and sentenced to pay a fine or serve time in prison; that is his punishment. The wages of sin is death; the punishment is over and above that.

The sin nature is personified by the Apostle Paul. He likens it to a cruel master, a merciless tyrant, and such it is. The unsaved are the bondslaves of sin. Paul writes, "Know ye not, that to whom ye yield yourselves servants to obey, his servants ye are to whom ye obey; whether of sin unto death, or of obedience unto righteousness? But God be thanked, that ye were the servants (bondslaves) of sin, but ye have obeyed from the heart that form of doctrine which was delivered you" (Rom. 6:16, 17).

A comparison of Romans 3:21-26 with Romans 6:6-10, will definitely reveal that the blood answers to "sins," and the Cross to "Sin."

This disposition to sin is the possession of all who have come into the world through natural generation—the one exception being our Lord Jesus Christ. Many have attempted to improve the sin nature by patching it up in one way or another, even to the extent of making it religious. Religious flesh is one of the greatest curses of the church today, if not the greatest.

This aspect of sin is responsible for all the terrible crimes that men are guilty of. "For out of the heart proceed evil thoughts, murders, adulteries, fornications, thefts, false witness, blasphemies" (Matt. 15:19). "Keep thy heart with all diligence; for out of it are the issues of life" (Prov. 4:23). "A man's heart deviseth his way" (Prov. 16:9). "For as he thinketh in his heart, so is he" (Prov. 23:7).

One is not responsible for possessing a sin nature, but one is responsible for the outworking of that nature when the age of accountability is reached.

In the light of this faithful testimony of Scripture concerning the sin nature inherited from Adam, it is difficult to understand how men, who say they believe the Bible to be the Word of God, can then believe that man is born into this world with what they term a "divine spark." God's testimony regarding man is one hundred per cent against such teaching.

When a person claims to have gotten rid of the sin nature, he thereby claims equality with the Lord Jesus Christ, and is according to the Word, deceived, for we read, "If we say that we have no sin, we deceive ourselves, and the truth is not in us" (I John 1:8).

Note that John writes his epistle to "my little children" and not to the unsaved, as many, if not all eradicationists contend. He does not say the believer *must* sin, but since he possesses a sin nature, he is liable to sin. The source of sin in the believer is the fallen nature inherited from Adam. In another section of the book we shall see what God has done with the sin nature.

Sin In Action

"All have sinned and come short of the glory of God" (Rom. 3:23). This is sin of commission and omission. It is against the revealed will of God—a failure to act in accordance with His infinitely holy and righteous character. This aspect of sin renders man a sinner in thought, word, and deed, when he reaches the age of accountability. It is in the Scriptures described by the following terms:

Transgression—This means a breaking over or the overstepping of the Law, which is God's boundary between good and evil.

"According to the multitude of thy tender mercies blot out my transgressions" (Psalm 51:1); "Neither transgressed I at any time thy commandment" (Luke 15:29). "For where no law is, there is no transgression" (Rom. 4:15); "Why do ye also transgress the commandment of God by your tradition?" (Matt. 15:3).

Man is a rebel by nature and that nature breaks out in open rebellion against God and His holy Law.

Iniquity—This is an act inherently wrong whether definitely forbidden or not. It gathers into itself the thought of perverseness, crookedness and that which is warped and bent out of shape.

"We have sinned, and have committed iniquity, and have done wickedly, and have rebelled, even by departing from thy precepts and from thy judgments" (Dan. 9:5).

"Who forgiveth all thine inquities: who healeth all thy diseases" (Psalm 103:3).

"And he laid it upon my mouth, and said, Lo, this hath touched thy lips; and thine iniquity is taken away, and thy sin is purged" (Isa. 6:7).

Error—This is a departure from that which is right in deed or in doctrine.

"Hereby know we the Spirit of Truth, and the spirit of error" (I John 4:6).

"Who can understand his errors" (Psalm 19:12).

Missing the Mark—This is a failure to measure up to the divine standard—God's character. "All have sinned and come short of the glory of God" (Rom. 3:23).

Trespass—This is against the infinitely holy and righteous character of God. It is an intrusion of self-will into the sphere of divine authority. God is outraged by every sin, whether it be that of a sinner, or a saint.

"And you, being dead in your sins and the uncircumcision of your flesh, hath he quickened together with him, having forgiven you all trespasses" (Col. 2:13).

Lawlessness—"Sin is lawlessness" (I John 3:4). Personal sins persisted in become lawlessness. It is spiritual anarchy.

Unbelief—"Of sin because they believe not on me" (John 16:9). "He that believeth on him is not condemned: but he that believeth not is condemned already, because he hath not believed in the name of the only begotten Son of God" (John 3:18).

Unbelief is an insult to the divine veracity. No wonder we are told that "without faith it is impossible to please him" (Heb. 11:6). It is the easily besetting sin (Heb. 12:1), and the one all condemning sin (John 16:9; 3:18).

Sin As a Judicial Reckoning

This is a dispensational aspect of sin, and is the result of the divine reckoning against the whole race.

Before the Cross there was a positional difference between the Jew and the Gentile. Morally there was no difference, because they both sprang from the same common stock and were sinners by imputation, in nature, and in practice.

By the judicial reckoning all were brought down to the same level and all differences between them were done away. This truth is summed up in the words of the Apostle Paul when he writes, "What then? Are we better? No, in no wise: for we have before proved both Jews and Gentiles, that they are all under sin" (Rom. 3:9); "But the scripture hath concluded all under sin, that the promise by faith of Jesus Christ might be given to them that believe" (Gal. 3:22).

When Paul says, "All are under sin," he does not mean that all have sinned in the same degree, or that all are guilty of the same crimes, for we know they are not. But he does mean that the best moralist is as much lost and undone as the one that is guilty of the worst of sins.

We do not say their punishment will be the same if they go out of this world in their lost condition, because the lost will be judged according to their works as we read, "And I saw the dead, great and small, standing before the throne. And the books were opened; and another book was opened, which is the book of life; and the dead were judged out of those things which were written in the books according to their works. And the sea gave up the dead which were in it; and death and hell (hades) delivered up the dead which were in them: and they were judged every man according to their works" (Rev. 20:12, 13).

We repeat that death in its every aspect is the "wages of sin," and the punishment is over and above that.

The judicial reckoning of sin also means that God absolutely refuses to credit man with any good works done before he is saved. We are saved by grace, and grace does not recognize any works as meritorious in salvation.

The positional difference, which obtained between the Circumcision and the Uncircumcision before the Cross, will be seen by a comparison of Rom. 9:4, 5 with Eph. 2:12. In Paul's letter to the Romans we read, "Who are Israelites; to whom pertaineth the adoption, and the glory, and the covenants, and the giving of the law, and the service of God, and the promises; whose are the fathers, and of whom as concerning the flesh Christ came, who is over all, God blessed for ever. Amen." To the Ephesians he writes, "That at that time ye were without Christ, being aliens from the commonwealth of Israel, and strangers from the covenants of promise, having no hope, and without God in the world."

The Jew had all the advantages and blessings; the Gentiles had nothing. Through the Cross this difference was removed. This does not mean that the Gentiles were raised to the level of the Jews, but rather that the Jews were placed on a level with the Gentiles; from the two classes, now on the same level, God saves all who believe on the Lord Jesus Christ, and makes of the two "one new man," which is the Church, the body of Christ.

This important truth is also found in the Gospels, and because it has been ignored by many, and denied by not a few, it has led to hopeless confusion — promises made to Israel as God's earthly people, have been transferred to the church.

The difference that obtained between the Jew and the Gentile is revealed in the words of our Lord when He commanded His disciples, saying, "Go not into the way of the Gentiles, and into a city of the Samaritans enter ye not: but go rather to the lost sheep of the house of Israel" (Matt. 10:5, 6). At another time Christ said, "I am not sent, but unto the lost sheep of the house of Israel" (Matt. 15:24).

Why were the Gentiles shut out in this way? This is a fair question. According to the Scriptures man had utterly failed during the first three dispensations: the first ended in wilful disobedience on the part of Adam and Eve (Gen. 3:1-7); the second ended in moral perversion (Gen. 6:1-8); and the third ended in organized rebellion (Gen. 11:1-4).

In the first chapter of Romans it is three times stated, "God gave them up" (Rom. 1:24, 26, 28), but however, not until they had completely turned away from Him. We read, "Because that, when they knew

God, they glorified him not as God, neither were thankful; but became vain in their imaginations, and their foolish heart was darkened. Professing themselves to be wise, they became fools, and changed the glory of the uncorruptible God into an image made like to corruptible man, and to birds, and fourfooted beasts, and creeping things" (Rom. 1:21-23). "Wherefore God gave them up."

Abraham lived amongst an idolatrous people when he was called to leave his country. We are told, "Joshua said unto all the people, Thus saith the LORD God of Israel, Your fathers dwelt on the other side of the flood (river) in old time, even Terah, the father of Abraham, and the father of Nachor: and they served other gods" (Joshua 24:2).

During the present dispensation of Grace, God does not deal with Israel as a nation. He deals with both Jew and Gentile alike as individuals. They are all "under sin," and all that are saved have been saved by grace, through faith, "Not by works of righteousness which we have done, but according to his mercy he saved us, by the washing of regeneration, and renewing of the Holy Ghost" (Titus 3:5).

"Who hath saved us, and called us with an holy calling, not according to our works, but according to his own purpose and grace, which was given us in Christ Jesus before the world began, but is now made manifest by the appearing of our Saviour Jesus Christ, who hath abolished death, and hath brought life and immortality to light through the gospel: whereunto I am appointed a preacher, and an apostle, and a teacher of the Gentiles" (II Tim. 1:9-11).

CHAPTER IV.

THE RESULT OF GOD'S JUDGMENT UPON ADAM'S ORIGINAL SIN

It is clearly revealed in the Scriptures that God came down in judgment and pronounced His righteous sentence upon Adam. We read, "For the judgment was by one to condemnation" (Rom. 5:16). Since this has to do with Adam's first sin, we are not concerned with the sins he committed after he became a sinner.

Some contend against this aspect of truth, and say that God came down only in love, seeking for Adam, just as He today seeks the lost. Yes, God is love, but do not forget that He also is a "consuming fire," and that "it is a fearful thing to fall into the hands of a living God." Remember, too, that every judgment results in either the condemnation or the acquittal of the accused one.

The extent of the penalty indicates the proportion of guilt. So, in the divine judgment upon Adam because of his sin, the proportion of his guilt is revealed in the following results:

1. Total Depravity

"Man, by his fall into a state of sin, hath wholly lost all ability of will to any spiritual good accompanying salvation; so as a natural man, being altogether averse from good, and dead in sin, is not able, by his own strength, to convert himself, or to prepare himself thereto" (Westminster Confession).

The doctrine of total depravity, which declares that all men are dead in sin, with no ability whatsoever with reference to that which is good, is not to the liking of the natural man, and especially not to the moralists. It does not mean that all men are equally bad, nor as bad as they could be. But it does mean that since the Fall, man rests under the curse of sin, that he is prompted by wrong principles, and that he is wholly unable to love God or to do anything that merits salvation. Concerning this Paul writes, "What then? Are we better than they? No, in no wise: for we have before proved both Jews and Gentiles, that they are under sin; as it is written, There is none righteous, no, not one: There is none that understandeth, there is none that seeketh after God. They are all gone out of the way, they are together become unprofitable; there is none that doeth good, no, not one. Their throat is an open sepulchre; with their tongues they have used deceit; the poison of asps is under their lips: whose mouth is full of cursing and bitterness: their feet are swift to shed blood: destruction and misery are in their ways: and the way of peace have they not known: there is no fear of God before their eyes" (Rom. 3:9-18). This is God's photograph of the unregenerate, and it is by no means a flattering one; but it is the one that is absolutely true.

Since the Fall, man has been utterly indisposed to that which is good, and wholly inclined to that which is evil. His will is biased against God, and instinctively and willingly he turns to that which is evil. His will is controlled by his sinful nature. There is much talk about the free-will of man, and the placing of man's will over against God's sovereign will. Man is a free agent, but when he possesses no will with reference to that which is holy, but only to that which is evil, it is manifest that the natural man possesses no ability to be willing to exercise holy volitions.

On this subject, Luther, in his "Bondage of the Will," declares, "Free-will is an empty term, whose reality is lost. And a lost liberty, according to my grammar, is no liberty at all."

The natural man can, through what is termed "common grace," be kind; he can love his family and his fellow men and so be a model citizen. He may give all his possessions for the benefit of his fellow men, and many other noble deeds may be credited to him; but they are all worthless, and in no way merit salvation, because these deeds are not of faith.

The unregenerate are in a state of rebellion against God. They must give up their rebellion and turn to God from their sins—the result of trusting in Christ for salvation. Saving faith is produced (by the Holy Spirit) in the individual, and is therefore to be classed as a gift of God. "But to him that worketh not, but believeth on him that justifieth the ungodly, his faith is counted for righteousness" (Rom. 4:5).

Our Lord said, "For a good tree bringeth not forth corrupt fruit; neither doth a corrupt tree bring forth good fruit. For every tree is known by his own fruit. For of thorns men do not gather figs, nor of a bramble bush gather they grapes" (Luke 6:43, 44).

Before the tree can bring forth good fruit it must be made good. So also, before a lost and guilty sinner can do any good deed that is acceptable in God's sight, he must be created anew in Christ Jesus. But, even then, it is not possible for him to produce any righteousness through his own efforts. If anything of value, in the sight of God, is to be produced, it must be wrought in him and not by him. We read, "For what the law could not do, in that it was weak through the flesh, God sending his own Son in the likeness of sinful flesh, and for sin, condemned sin in the flesh: That the righteousness of the law might be fulfilled in us, who walk not after the flesh, but after the Spirit" (Rom. 8:3, 4).

To the Philippians Paul writes, "Wherefore, my beloved, as ye have always obeyed, not as in my presence only, but now much more in my absence, work out your own salvation with fear and trembling. For it is God which worketh in you both to will and to do of his good pleasure" (Phil. 2:12, 13).

"But I labored more abundantly than they all; yet not I, but the grace of God which was with me" (I Cor. 15:10).

2. Enslavement to Sin and to Satan

On this subject there is much said in the Word. Our Lord says, "Whosoever committeth sin is the servant (bondslave) of sin" (John 8:34). Paul writes, "Know ye not, that to whom ye yield yourselves as servants (bondmen) to obey, his servants ye are whom ye obey." "Ye were the servants of sin" (Rom. 6:16, 17). "But I am carnal, sold under sin" (Rom. 7:14).

"And you hath he quickened, who were dead in trespasses and sins; wherein in time past ye walked according to the course of this world (age), according to the prince of the power of the air, the spirit that now worketh in the children of disobedience: Among whom also we all had our conversation in times past in the lusts of our flesh and of the mind; and were by nature the children of wrath even as others" (Eph. 2:1-3).

"Is this the man that made the earth to tremble, that did shake kingdoms; that made the world as a wilderness, and destroyed the cities thereof; *that opened not the house of his prisoners*" (Isa. 14:16, 17).

"And that they may recover themselves out of the snare of the devil, who are taken captive by him at his will" (II Tim. 2:26).

"Forasmuch then as the children are partakers of flesh and blood, he also himself likewise took part of the same; that through death he might destroy him that had the power of death, that is, the devil; and deliver them who through fear of death were all their lifetime subject to bondage" (Heb. 2:14, 15).

"While they promise them liberty, they themselves are the servants (bondmen) of corruption: for of whom a man is overcome, of the same is he brought into bondage" (II Peter 2:19).

"Can the Ethiopian change his skin, or the leopard his spots? Then may ye also do good that are accustomed to do evil" (Jer. 13:23).

"For when ye were the servants (bondmen) of sin, ye were free from righteousness" (Rom. 6:20).

Redemption implies bondage. The words employed in the original text reveal this very definitely. If you are fortunate enough to possess a Scofield Reference Bible (if you do not, sell your hat and buy one) you will find a most helpful explanation of this truth in Dr. Scofield's comment on Rom. 3:24.

3. A Blinded Mind

Knowing that man is a captive of his, and unable to do anything to merit salvation, and that it is the Gospel that is the power of God unto salvation, Satan has blinded the minds of the unsaved. We are told, "But if our gospel be hid, it is hid to them that are lost: In whom the god of this world (age) hath blinded the minds of them which believe not, lest the light of the glorious gospel of Christ, who is the image of God, should shine unto them" (II Cor. 4:3, 4).

Herein is revealed one of the most fundamental truths in relation to all evangelistic efforts. Though Satan is not omniscient, he does know many things, and one of them is that the Gospel of Grace is the power of God unto salvation to every one that believeth. He therefore does everything possible to keep lost sinners from hearing the Gospel. He has placed a veil over their minds so that they do not understand the good news of salvation. Note, "For the preaching of the cross is to them that perish foolishness; but unto us which are saved it is the power of God" (I Cor. 1:18). They may be perfectly normal with reference to temporal things; but it is foolishness to them that there is salvation in believing in Another One and what He has done.

It is reasonable to believe that one is saved by good works. But God says, No, "For by grace are ye saved through faith; and that not of yourselves: it is the gift of God: not of works, lest any man should boast" (Eph. 2:8, 9).

Until this veil is removed, man cannot intelligently exercise saving faith. The only one that can remove this veil is the Holy Spirit. He uses the Gospel of Grace in his convicting ministry. Of this our Lord says, "Nevertheless I tell you the truth; it is expedient for you that I go away: for if I go not away, the Comforter will not come unto you; but if I depart, I will send him unto you. And when he is come, he will reprove the world of sin, and of righteousness, and of judgment: Of sin, because they believe not on me; Of righteousness, because I go to my Father, and ye see me no more; Of judgment, because the prince of this world is judged" (John 16:7-11).

These verses contain the very core of the Gospel of Grace, which is the power of God unto salvation.

The word translated "reprove" means to unveil or to bring to light the true facts regarding God's plan of salvation.

Much harm has been done by forcing men to make decisions before this work of the Spirit has been accomplished. When it is accomplished there will be no need of employing the unscriptural high-pressure methods that have been resorted to in order to get some kind of results.

We can trust the Holy Spirit to do His work in this respect as in every ministry of His in relation to the salvation of lost sinners.

4. Corrupted Affections

"For this cause God gave them up unto vile affections: for even their women did change the natural use into that which is against nature: And likewise also the men, leaving the natural use of the woman, burned in their lust one toward another; men with men working that which is unseemly, and receiving in themselves that recompence of their error which was meet. And even as they did not like to retain God in their knowledge, God gave them up over to a reprobate mind, to do those things which are not convenient" (Rom. 1:26-28).

This is evidently a summing up of the various incidents related in the Old Testament Scriptures. But we find many of these things spoken of in the New Testament, and about those "having a form of godliness, but denying the power thereof."

5. The Penalty of Sin—Death

"But of the tree of the knowledge of good and evil thou shalt not eat of it; for in the day that thou eatest thereof thou shalt surely die" (Gen. 2:17).

"Wherefore, as through one man sin entered into

the world, and death by sin; and so death passed upon all men, for that all have sinned" (Rom. 5:12).

"For since by man came death, by man came also the resurrection of the dead. For as in Adam all die, even so in Christ shall all be made alive" (I Cor. 15:21, 22).

When Adam sinned the seeds of mortality were sown in his constitution, and in the course of time he died. All of Adam's children were born after he was expelled from the garden of Eden, after he became a sinner. We read, "Adam lived an hundred and thirty years, and he begat a son in his own likeness, after his image; and called his name Seth" (Gen. 5:3).

Man is born dead in trespasses and sins. He is dead spiritually; his body is mortal. He is subject to physical death as soon as he enters this world. He is also under the sentence of the second death, the lake of fire, which is eternal separation from God. "But the fearful, and unbelieving, and the abominable, and murderers, and whoremongers, and sorcerers, and idolaters, and all liars, shall have their part in the lake which burneth with fire and brimstone: which is the second death" (Rev. 21:8).

6. Creation Subjected to Vanity

When He had finished His work in creation, "God saw everything that he had made, and, behold, it was very good" (Gen. 1:31).

In the works of man, language has been strained to its limits to portray the beauty of creation, and especially the Garden of Eden.

The Psalmist says, "The heavens declare the glory of God; and the firmament showeth his handiwork" (Psalm 19:1). "All things were created by him, and for him" (Col. 1:16).

"God pronounced His work good, because sin had not entered to mar its beauty, and disturb its order. The heavens were resplendent with the glory of their Maker, and the earth was full of His praise. The trees and the herbs of the field displayed His wisdom and goodness; the inferior animals were perfect in their kind; and man placed at their head, was enlightened by reason, and adorned with every moral excellence. There never was so lovely a sight as our world bearing the recent impress of the hand which fashioned it. The memory of its original state conveyed down by tradition, suggested to the heathen poets their descriptions of the golden age, when earth spontaneously yielded its fruits, the manners of its inhabitants were simple and virtuous, and life flowed on smoothly in innocence and peace. The whole creation declared the glory of God; and man as the priest of nature, gave a voice to its silent homage, and offered up to the universal Parent, the pure sacrifices of adoration and thanksgiving." (Dick)

Surely, it must have been a most beautiful scene to behold! Even the animal life was beautiful within its realm. Many beautiful scenes have been produced by the ingenuity and skill of man, but none can ever approach the original creation in its pristine beauty.

This wonderful creation which was made for the Son of God and the sons of God was plunged into darkness and ruin through the one act of disobedience of the first man, Adam. Because of this, his one sin, God said, "Cursed is the ground for thy sake; in sorrow shalt thou eat of it all the days of thy life; thorns also and thistles shall it bring forth to thee; and thou shalt eat of the herb of the field; in the sweat of thy face shalt thou eat bread, till thou return unto the ground; for out of it wast thou taken: for dust thou art, and unto dust shalt thou return" (Gen. 3:17-19).

Paul describes the present condition of the earth as "the bondage of corruption." He says also that creation groans under the pains of unavailing labor, pangs that bring forth nothing. The blight of sin rests upon the whole creation, and will continue to do so until the present order is by power redeemed and delivered "into the liberty of the glory of the children of God."

There are many Old Testament Scriptures that speak about the redeemed earth and the conditions that will then obtain. We read, "The wilderness and the solitary place shall be glad for them; and the desert shall rejoice, and blossom as the rose. It shall blossom abundantly, and rejoice even with joy and singing: the glory of Lebanon shall be given unto it, the excellency of Carmel and Sharon, they shall see the glory of the LORD, and the excellency of our God" (Isa. 35:1, 2).

The whole chapter (Isa. 35) is descriptive of the redeemed earth, such as it will be during the Kingdom Age, when our Lord will occupy the throne of His father David, and rule over the house of Jacob.

SECTION TWO

THE LAW

CHAPTER V.

THE LAW

Introductory Remarks

In section one we have definitely and positively seen that man's condition apart from the divine remedy for sin is a state of utter helplessness and hopelessness—a situation beyond human repair.

Through the years, men, conscious of their lost condition and undone estate, have tried various remedies for their plight. These attempts bring to mind the words of the Apostle Paul when he says, "For they being ignorant of God's righteousness, and going about to establish their own righteousness, have not submitted themselves unto the righteousness of God" (Rom. 10:3). This he says about his own kinsmen, the Jews: but many others are occupied with the same futile efforts.

Today, to some under conviction of sin, comes an exhortation to "forget about it, you are not so bad that you need be so concerned." Another one says, "You must assert your better self (whatever that is); fight against the evil you are tempted to do." "Clean up your past and start all over again," is the advice of many. Some one else suggests that the troubled one busy himself with social service.

Along comes another, a very solemn appearing one, who suggests to the afflicted one that, if he but spend more time saying his prayers and engaging in religious activities, all will be well.

Many are the remedies prepared and advocated by all kinds of religious quacks.

A Christian to many of these is one who has been born in a so-called Christian land. Others, in an effort to become Christians, endeavor to imitate Christ; to be His followers, to stand for His ideals and to follow His example.

Perhaps the most common of all is the old, old remedy, "Do the best you can to keep the Ten Commandments, and to live according to the Sermon on the Mount."

This seems very reasonable and appeals to the flesh, because it gives man something to glory in, but not before God. This is but an attempt to establish a righteousness of his own, and in so doing, he does not submit to the righteousness of God.

Because of the almost universal confusion and uncertainty prevalent today concerning the true and scriptural teaching about the Law, it is of the utmost importance and very necessary to be informed as to its true character and purpose.

When the Apostle Paul writes, "Moreover the law entered," he implies that there was a time when there was no Law; when he writes, "It was added because of transgressions, till the seed should come to whom the promise was made" (Gal. 3:19), he reveals that the Law was a temporary institution. We shall consider this subject under four sub-divisions.

Conditions Before the Law

When Adam sinned in the garden he transgressed the express commandment of God. That is why the Apostle Paul refers to his original sin as a transgression, which means an overstepping of the Law, the divine boundary between good and evil. He also makes it known that there was no Law from Adam to Moses. He says, "Nevertheless death reigned from Adam to Moses, even over them that had not sinned after the similitude of Adam's transgression, who is the figure of him that was to come" (Rom. 5:14). Some see in this statement of the apostle a reference to infants only. However in another place Paul says, "For where no law is, there is no transgression" (Rom. 4:15).

That God and His demands were the same we do not question for a moment; also that sin was as sinful from Adam to Moses, as it now is and ever will be, we are sure no one will question. God cannot demand less during one age than in another. He is immutable; His infinitely perfect character does not change. When we say there was a time when there was no Law, we refer to the Mosaic Law.

The Law in any form whatsoever is a reflection of His inherent Law—His infinitely holy and righteous character.

To prove that Adam's original sin was imputed to his posterity, Paul says, "Nevertheless death reigned from Adam to Moses, even over them that had not sinned after the similitude of Adam's transgression."

The Nature of the Law

"But we know that the law is good, if a man use it lawfully; knowing this, that the law is not made for a righteous man, but for the lawless and disobedient, for the ungodly and for sinners, for unholy and profane, for murderers of fathers and murderers of mothers, for manslayers, for whoremongers, for them that defile themselves with mankind, for menstealers, for liars, for perjured persons, and if there be any other thing that is contrary to sound doctrine" (I Tim. 1:8-10).

Wherefore the law is holy, and the commandment holy, and just, and good. For we know that the law is spiritual: but I am carnal, sold under sin" (Rom. 7:12, 14).

The Law is unrelated to faith. Paul writes, "This only would I learn of you, Received ye the Spirit by works of the law, or by the hearing of faith?" (Gal. 3:2). Paul wrote the Epistle to the Galatians as God's answer to legalism.

Law and works are inseparably linked together; Israel's blessings were conditional. When Moses restated the Law, he said to the people, "Now these are the commandments, the statutes, and the judgments, which the LORD your God commanded to teach you, that ye might do them in the land whither ye go to possess it: that thou mightest fear the LORD thy God, to keep all his statutes and his commandments, which I command thee, thou, and thy son, and thy son's son, all the days of thy life; and that thy days may be prolonged" (Deut. 6:1, 2).

In the Epistle to the Galatians we read, "Knowing that a man is not justified by the works of the law, but by the faith of Jesus Christ, even we have believed in Jesus Christ, that we might be justified by the faith of Christ, and not by the works of the law: for by the works of the law shall no flesh be justified" (Gal. 2:16). "For as many as are of the works of the law are under the curse: for it is written, Cursed is every one that continueth not in all things which are written in the book of the law to do them" (Gal. 3:10).

The Law was given to Israel as God's covenant people, and not to make them such. Before the Law was given Israel was under grace. God said to them, "I bare you on eagle's wings, and brought you unto myself" (Exodus 19:4). The only responsibility imposed upon man under the Abrahamic covenant was that he remain in the place of blessing—the Land, Palestine.

God proposed the Law, and Israel accepted it. They said, "All that the LORD hath spoken we will do" (Exodus 19:8), thus taking an impossible merit system in exchange for pure grace. It was given to that nation as God's rule of life for His earthly people.

Under the Law God said, "If you will be good, I will bless you." Under grace He says, "I have blessed you, now you be good."

The Law was given by Moses, who also was its chief exponent (John 1:17). It came by the disposition of angels (Acts 7:53). Paul says, "It was ordained by angels in the hand of a mediator" (Gal. 3:19).

As it was given the first time, the Law contained only the Ten Commandments. Have you ever stopped to consider what would have happened to Israel if the Law had remained in its original form? Without any provision in the Law for the forgiveness of sins, the nation would soon have perished.

When Moses received the Law the second time there was added to it the means by which a transgressor could be forgiven. It was in three parts: the Ten Commandments, expressing the holy and righteous will of God (Ex. 20:1-26); the judgments, governing the civil or social life of Israel (Ex. 21:1—24:11); the ordinances, governing the religious life of the covenant people (Ex. 24:12—31:18).

Remember the Law was, and is, as inflexible as God's infinitely holy and righteous character. Under the Law it was not a matter of trying to keep the Law. The one who did not obey it had to suffer the consequence. The ordinances prescribed the offering the sinning Israelite was to provide when he sinned. But there were sins for which there was no offering or sacrifice. There were some things from which man could not be justified by the Law of Moses (Acts 13:39).

CHAPTER VI.

WHAT THE LAW COULD NOT DO

We have seen that the Law is holy, just, good, and spiritual; also we are absolutely sure that it has accomplished its God-given purpose. But note some things it could not do:

1. It Prescribed Duty, But Provided No Motive

The Ten Commandments disclose man's duty toward God, and also his duty to his fellow men.

In the Judgments, the portion of the Law that governed the civil life of Israel and in the Ordinances which governed the religious life of the nation, one finds duty prescribed in the minutest detail.

However, the Law provided no motive to do what was commanded, but rather excited the passions of the natural man. Paul says, "For when we were in the flesh, the motions of sins, which were by the law, did work in our members to bring forth fruit unto death" (Rom. 7:5); "But sin, taking occasion by the commandment, wrought in me all manner of concupiscence. For without the law sin was dead" (Rom. 7:8).

2. It Demanded Obedience, But Could Not Make Man Obedient

"For not the hearers of the law are just before God, but the doers of the law shall be justified" (Rom. 2:13). Since no one ever did do the Law, no one was ever justified by it.

This obedience had to be no less than one hundred per cent perfect. God could not accept anything less. Some one has said, "The law is a stern taskmaster," and so it is. But although the Law demanded obedience of man, it could not make him obedient. Forbid a child to do something which he has never thought of doing, and at once he will long to do it. A story is told about a man in a city of Italy, who had never been beyond the confines of the city in which he was born and had lived all his life. This man declared that he had no desire whatsoever to leave the city. The ruling governor heard about the man and what he had said, and sent him a strict order forbidding him ever to leave his beloved city. From that time on to his dying day he wanted to go. "But sin, taking occasion by the commandment, wrought in me all manner of concupiscence."

3. The Law Required Righteousness, But Could Not Make Man Righteous

"For what the law could not do, in that it was weak through the flesh, God sending his own Son in the likeness of sinful flesh, and for sin, condemned sin in the flesh: that the righteousness of the law might be fulfilled in us, who walk not after the flesh, but after the Spirit" (Rom. 8:3, 4).

"For Christ is the end of the law for righteousness to every one that believeth" (Rom. 10:4).

The Mosaic Law as the rule of life for God's earthly people demanded righteousness and that no less than one hundred per cent perfect. The Law was absolutely inflexible in its demands, and not a sort of an accordion affair that could be adjusted to suit the individual. It could not justify nor make man righteous, for we read, "Knowing that a man is not justified by the works of the law, but by the faith of Jesus Christ, that we might be justified by the faith of Christ, and not by the works of the law: for by the works of the law shall no flesh be justified" (Gal. 2:16); "I do not frustrate the grace of God: for if righteousness come by the law, then Christ is dead in vain" (Gal. 2:21); "Therefore by the deeds of the law there shall no flesh be justified in his sight" (Rom. 3:20).

4. The Law Revealed Sin, But Could Not Remove It

Just as a ray of sunlight will reveal dust on a piece of furniture, so the Law reveals sin. The brighter the sunlight, the clearer the dust is revealed. This is also true concerning the Law, for we are told, "What shall we say then? Is the law sin? God forbid. Nay, I had not known sin, but by the law: for I had not known lust, except the law had said, Thou shalt not covet" (Rom. 7:7).

The Law no more creates the sin than the sunlight creates the dust, Neither can the Law remove the sin any more than the sunlight the dust. But thank God, there is a mighty power that can remove sin—"Where sin abounded, grace did much more abound." "Unto him that loved us, and washed us from our sins in his own blood" (Rev. 1:5).

5. The Law Enslaved Men, But Could Not Set Them Free

"Stand fast therefore in the liberty wherewith Christ hath made us free, and be not entangled again with the yoke of bondage" (Gal. 5:1).

The Epistle to the Galatians is God's answer to every form of legalism. Judaizing teachers had come into the churches in Galatia teaching them that it was necessary to add the works of the Law to the finished work of Christ on the Cross. Again and again we find it stated in the Scriptures that legalism is an enslaving yoke. The message of Galatians is very much needed in our time. Everywhere one finds the Lord's people struggling under the "yoke of bondage." In Gal. 4:9 we read, "But now, after that ye have known God, or rather are known of God, how turn ye again to the weak and beggarly elements, whereunto ye desire again to be in bondage?" In the Book of Acts we read what Peter declared when the apostles and the elders met in council at Jerusalem. "And the apostles and elders came together for to consider of this matter (circumcision). And when there had been much disputing, Peter rose up, and said unto them, Men and brethren, ye know how that a good while ago God made choice among us, that the Gentiles by my mouth should hear the word of the Gospel, and believe. And God, which knoweth the hearts, bare them witness, giving them the Holy Ghost, even as he did unto us; and put no difference between us and them, purifying their hearts by faith. Now therefore why tempt ye God, to put a yoke upon the neck of the disciples, which neither our fathers nor we were able to bear? But we believe that through the grace of the Lord Jesus Christ we shall be saved, even as they" (Acts 15:6-11).

These verses plainly teach that the Law enslaves men, but there is no word that tells us that the Law could liberate those in bondage. Not one had fulfilled the high and holy demands of the Law for the Law is an impossible merit system.

Legalism denies the finished work of Christ on the Cross. It robs the believer of his liberty and hinders him in his spiritual progress. It produces stunted Christians.

6. The Law Condemned to Death the Best of Men, But Could Not Give Life

When the Apostle Paul asks the question, "Who is

he that condemneth?" (Rom. 8:34), he evidently has the Law in mind. We have seen in a previous chapter that God's judgment upon Adam's original sin resulted in the condemnation of all men. Then the Law came in and confirmed this judgment and its results. James says, "For whosoever shall keep the whole law, and yet offend in one point, he is guilty of all" (James 2:10).

When a certain lawyer stood up and tempted our Lord, asking, "Master, what shall I do to inherit eternal life?" (Luke 10:25), he was by the Lord brought face to face with the Law and its demands. He answered correctly when he was questioned concerning the Law, and to his answer the Lord replied, "This do, and thou shalt live."

He had not met the requirements of the Law; he could not meet them and so could not receive life through the Law. We are told, "For if there had been a law given which could have given life, verily righteousness should have been by the law" (Gal. 3:21).

7. The Law Made Nothing Perfect

The Law prescribed duty, but provided no motive; it demanded obedience, but could not make man obedient; it required righteousness, but could not justify; it revealed sin, but could not remove it; it enslaved men, but could not set them free; it condemned and killed the best of men, but could not give life. No wonder the apostle says, "The law made nothing perfect."

There was nothing wrong with the Law. It was as perfect as the author of it. Paul reveals the reason for the inability of the Law when he says, "For what the law could not do, in that it was weak through the flesh." The trouble was with the flesh and not with the Law. The flesh is powerless for that which is good.

The natural man is a total failure with reference to righteousness.

I may have a lever strong enough to raise an object weighing many tons, but if my fulcrum is of cardboard I cannot accomplish my task though the lever be perfect.

CHAPTER VII.

"WHEREFORE THEN SERVETH THE LAW?"

Since it is so clearly revealed in the Scriptures that the Law could not justify, save, nor make man good—in other words that the Law was not given as a cure or remedy for man's lost condition, many ask, "Why then the Law?"

Remember, it was given as the rule of life to a people already chosen by God. It was not given to give life nor to make them a covenant nation.

When God proposed the Law, Israel said, "All that the LORD hath spoken we will do." Did they do it? No. Could they do it? No, never. Did God expect them to do it? No. Why then the Law?

According to the Scriptures, the Law was given for certain specific purposes. Note some of them:

1. To Give the Knowledge of Sin

The enormity and heinousness of sin are made conspicuous by the Law, inasmuch as sin makes even that which is in itself good, an incentive to evil. We read, "But sin, taking occasion by the commandment, wrought in me all manner of concupiscence" (Rom. 7:8). Note carefully the faithful testimony of the following verses of Scripture: "Moreover the law entered, that the offence might abound" (Rom. 5:20); "Nay, I had not known sin, but by the law: for I had not known lust, except the law had said, Thou shalt not covet" (Rom. 7:7); "That sin by the commandment might become exceeding sinful" (Rom. 7:13); "For by the law is the knowledge of sin" (Rom. 3:20).

Paul says, "For without the law sin was dead" (Rom. 7:8). It was through the Law that he discovered how very much alive sin was. Apart from the knowledge of the true purpose of the Law, sin was apparently inactive and unobserved and he was very much pleased with himself as his words in Phil. 3:6 reveal. There he says, "Touching the righteousness which is in the law, blameless." This is what he refers to when he says, "For I was alive without the law once: but when the commandment came, sin revived, and I died" (Rom. 7:9).

Note the four results of the coming in of the commandment, when he, Paul, saw the holy and spiritual character of the Law: it excited his evil passions (Rom. 7:5); it produced the knowledge of sin (Rom. 7:7); "For sin, taking occasion by the commandment, deceived me" (Rom. 7:11); the Law slew him (Rom. 7:11). "For I through the law am dead to the law" (Gal. 2:19).

2. That Every Mouth May Be Stopped

Man likes to be under the Law because it gives him something to glory in, something to boast about—not before God, but before man.

The incident of the rich young ruler related in the Gospels (Matt. 19:16-22; Mark 10:17-22; Luke 18:18-23), serves well to illustrate this purpose of the Law. We see here one who, as he himself declared, had observed every point of the Law from his youth up; yet concerned about his spiritual state, he came to Christ earnestly seeking to perfect his ways. He approached Christ on legal ground, saying, "Good Master, what must *I do* to inherit eternal life?" Christ answered the young man by referring him to the Law. In answer to the young man's second question, "What lack I yet?" Christ showed him that he had not fully kept the Law. Neither was he ready and willing to do so, for he went away sorrowful—silenced by the Law.

Note that the young man asked what he should do to *inherit* eternal life. What we inherit belongs to us by right and title; it is legally ours. No one inherits eternal life; it is the gift of God's grace.

Another incident shows how those appealing to the Law were silenced by it. "And the scribes and Pharisees brought unto him a woman taken in adultery; and when they had set her in the midst, they say unto him, Master, this woman was taken in adultery, in the very act. Now Moses in the law commanded us, that such should be stoned: but what sayest thou?" (John 8:3-5). After He had stooped down and written on the ground, He said, "He that is without sin among you, let him first cast a stone at her" (John 8:7). Then when He had again stooped down and written on the ground, the woman's accusers were silenced. We are told, "And they which heard it, being convicted by their own conscience, went out one by one, beginning at the eldest, even unto the last: and Jesus was left alone, and the woman standing in the midst" (John 8:9).

3. The Law Was Given To Bring Man Under Judgment to God

"Now we know that what things soever the law saith, it saith to them who are under the law: that every mouth may be stopped, and all the world may become guilty before God" (Rom. 3:19).

We have seen that the Law detects sin, and reveals it in its true character, and that it strips a man of his own righteousness, and silences his mouth.

Here we see the sinner as a criminal at the bar of justice, with no one to plead his cause. He is adjudged guilty of the greatest crime in the Universe—SIN. No excuses for past failures avail, and no promises for future reform are considered. He stands there a helpless, hopeless, and speechless criminal; and but for the mercy of God would be forever banished from His presence.

4. The Law Was Added Because of Transgressions

"It was added for the sake of defining sin" (Weymouth). The Law defines sin, and gives to it the character of transgression. "Because the law worketh wrath: for where no law is there is no transgression" (Rom. 4:15). Adam's original sin was a transgression. He had a definite command to refrain from eating of the tree of the knowledge of good and evil. That is why Paul says, "Them that had not sinned after the similitude of Adam's transgression" (Rom. 5:14).

In a certain town there was no law against riding a horse on the sidewalks. Later, a law was passed against such an act. It was just as dangerous to pedestrians and just as injurious to the walk before the law was passed as afterwards. But while it was an offence before, it was not a transgression until there was an express commandment to be broken. So sin was in the world before the Law was given, but it was not a transgression until after the entrance of the Law. It came in to reveal and not to remove sin; not to keep from sin, but because sin had already entered.

5. The Law Was Given To Curse and Condemn

"Behold, I set before you this day a blessing and a curse; a blessing, if ye obey the commandments of the LORD your God, which I command you this day: and a curse, if ye will not obey the commandments of the

LORD your God, but turn aside out of the way which I command you this day, to go after other gods, which ye have not known" (Deut. 11:26-28).

Though Israel had promised to do all that the LORD had spoken, she was not able to do it, and was therefore under the curse and condemnation of the Law.

Regarding the Law and its ministration the Apostle Paul says, "For if the ministration of condemnation be glory" (II Cor. 3:9). This he says about the Law engraved with letters on stone—the Ten Commandments —and not the ceremonial Law as some would have us believe. To the Galatians he writes, "For as many as are of the works of the law are under the curse: for it is written, Cursed is every one that continueth not in all things which are written in the book of the law to do them" (Gal. 3:10); "Christ hath redeemed us from the curse of the law, being made a curse for us: for it is written, Cursed is every one that hangeth on a tree" (Gal. 3:13).

6. The Law Was Given To Minister Death

"But if the ministration of death, written and engraven in stones, was glorious, so that the children of Israel could not stedfastly behold the face of Moses for the glory of his countenance, which glory was to be done away" (II Cor. 3:7). "The letter killeth" (II Cor. 3:6).

"For I was alive without the law once: but when the commandment came, sin revived, and I died. And the commandment, which was ordained to life, I found to be unto death. For sin, taking occasion by the commandment, deceived me, and by it slew me" (Rom. 7:9-11). And, "For I through the law am dead to the law, that I might live unto God" (Gal. 2:19). When Paul's words in Romans 7:10 are rendered, "And the commandment was ordained to life" it is evident that the words "was ordained" have been added by the translators because they are in italics. From the whole body of truth regarding the Law we know that the Law was not ordained to life, but to death.

With reference to when and where the Law slew Saul of Tarsus men are not agreed. Some say it was when he was on the way to Damascus to persecute the believers there. Others contend that it was when he was alone with the Lord in the Arabian Desert.

But one place is revealed where it could and did actually come to pass; that place was the Cross. It was on the Cross that "our old man was crucified." It was there that the Apostle Paul and all other true believers were slain by the Law.

We have already seen that the Law could not give life, but could only curse, condemn and kill. Therefore the believer is dead to the Law, and it was the Law itself which killed him. He is dead to the Law, not through suicide, but through execution. We are told, "That if one died for all, then were all dead" (II Cor. 5:14).

7. The Law Was Given To Be a Tutor unto Christ.

"Wherefore the law was our schoolmaster to bring us unto Christ" (Gal. 3:24).

Some consider this ministry of the Law in relation to Israel to be practically that of a truant officer conducting Israel to Christ.

SECTION THREE

CHRIST—THE SECOND MAN

CHAPTER VIII.

THE INCARNATION

Introductory Remarks

In our previous studies we have seen that sin entered the world through one man, that Adam's original sin was not mere lawlessness in character, but actual transgression, and that his original sin is imputed to every member of the Adamic race, so that all are constituted sinners.

It has also been demonstrated that man has no ability whatsoever to redeem himself, or to do any righteous deed that in any way merits salvation. His life as a sinner counts for nothing but sin in the sight of God. With reference to righteousness, man is a total failure. All his good deeds are as "filthy rags." He is always evil with no compensating good whatsoever.

The Law was given, but not as a cure or remedy for man's lost condition. Instead of being a means of bringing man back to God, it made his case all the more hopeless, because it clearly revealed his inability to measure up to the high and holy demands of an infinitely righteous God.

On this dark background God paints His marvelous story of redeeming love. "God so loved the world, that he gave his only begotten Son, that whosoever believeth in him should not perish, but have everlasting life."

It may appear to some from what we have seen in the preceding chapters, that God was defeated. But such is not the case. God could not be defeated for, "He worketh all things after the counsel of his own will."

We have noted that man's estate as a sinner is beyond repair as far as human help goes. Yes, it is so bad that instead of attempting to patch up the old Adamic line, God starts an entirely new thing by putting forth "the Second Man"—the Lord from heaven.

The Incarnation

"For what the law could not do, in that it was weak through the flesh, God sending his own Son in the likeness of sinful flesh, and for sin, condemned sin in the flesh" (Rom. 8:3).

What the Law could not do—justify, save, nor make man good—God could, and did do, when He sent His own Son into the world.

When sin entered the world, God at once announced the coming of the "Seed of the woman"—the Redeemer. Of Him and His coming it was by the Old Testament prophets predicted that He should be both God and man, divine and human. We read, "For unto us a child is born, unto us a Son is given" (Isa. 9:6). "A child is born" speaks of His humanity; as man He began to be when He was born in Bethlehem. "A Son is given" tells of His deity; as God He always was. His coming into the world was a miracle, as we will see more fully in another connection.

"But when the fulness of time was come, God sent forth his Son, made of a woman, made under the law" (Gal. 4:4).

The Biblical Reasons for the Incarnation

1. *The Son of God Became Incarnate To Reveal God to Man.* "No man hath seen God at any time; the only begotten Son, which is in the bosom of the Father, he hath declared him" (John 1:18). The word translated "declared" means "to lead out," "to make visible." God in His essential being is invisible. Concerning Him we read, "Who only hath immortality, dwelling in the light which no man can approach unto; whom no man hath seen, nor can see: to whom be honour and power everlasting. Amen" (I Tim. 6:16).

Christ came in the flesh that He might bring God within the range of human vision. This He did so perfectly that He could say, "He that hath seen me hath seen the Father" (John 14:9).

He came in the flesh that He might make God known as Father. He said, "I thank thee, O Father, Lord of heaven and earth, because thou hast hid these things from the wise and the prudent, and hast revealed them unto babes. Even so, Father; for so it seemed good in thy sight. All things are delivered unto me of my Father: and no man knoweth the Son, but the Father; neither knoweth any man the Father, save the Son, and he to whomsoever the Son will reveal him" (Matt. 11:25-27). Note the blessed result of knowing God as Father—"And ye shall find rest to your souls." Have you so learned to know Him? If not, listen to the words of our Lord, "Come unto me, all ye that labour and are heavy laden, and I will give you rest. Take my yoke upon you, and learn of me; for I am meek and lowly in heart: and ye shall find rest to your souls. For my yoke is easy, and my burden is light" (Matt. 11:28-30).

Christ came in the flesh to manifest the love of

God. Sometime ago I decided to make a study of God's love. In vain I searched the first four books of the Bible for some direct reference to the love of God. But when I turned to the New Testament I was even more surprised. I found that the first direct reference to God's love is John 3:16. (There is but an incidental allusion to God's love in the Gospel according to Luke.) Since "God is Love" we know that He loved, and still loves with an everlasting love. The measure of God's love is revealed in the letter to the Romans, where we read, "For when we were yet without strength, in due time Christ died for the ungodly. For scarcely for a righteous man will one die: yet peradventure for a good man some would even dare to die. But God commendeth His love toward us, in that, while we were yet sinners, Christ died for us. Much more then, being now justified by his blood, we shall be saved from wrath through him. For if, when we were enemies, we were reconciled to God by the death of his Son, much more being reconciled we shall be saved by his life" (Rom. 5:6-10).

Christ came in the flesh to enthrone grace. "For ye know the grace of our Lord Jesus Christ, that though he was rich, yet for your sakes he became poor, that ye through his poverty might be rich" (II Cor. 8:9); "For the grace of God that bringeth salvation hath appeared to all men, teaching us that, denying ungodliness and worldly lusts, we should live soberly, and righteously, and godly, in this present world (age); looking for that blessed hope, and the glorious appearing of the great God and our Saviour Jesus Christ" (Titus 2:11-13). "Grace and truth came by Jesus Christ" (John 1:17).

2. *The Son of God Became Incarnate in Order That He Might Reveal Man.* In the Gospel records are revealed the moral glories of our Lord—what He,

during the days of His flesh, was as God's ideal man—and as such He is the example for the believer. Peter says, "For even hereunto were ye called: because Christ also suffered for us, leaving us an example, that ye should follow in his steps" (I Peter 2:21). In this same line of truth Paul writes, "Let this mind be in you, which was also in Christ Jesus" (Phil. 2:5).

According to the Apostle John, "He that saith he abideth in him ought himself also so to walk, even as he walked" (I John 2:6).

While here on earth among men, our Lord walked in the light; He walked in perfect love; He walked in righteousness; He walked in the power of the anointing and in total dependency upon the Holy Spirit.

Following His example does not save. It is for the saved ones only that He is the example.

3. *The Son of God Became Incarnate To Be the Mediator Between God and Man.* We read, "For there is one God, and one mediator between God and men, the man Christ Jesus" (I Tim. 2:5).

A mediator is one who intervenes between two persons at variance. By the entrance of sin into the world, man and God were separated so that mediation between them has ever since been a necessity.

Moses was the mediator of the covenant which God made with Israel at Sinai; therefore, the Law is said to have been given "in the hand of a mediator."

Job recognized the need of a mediator when he said, "For he is not a man, as I am, that I should answer him, and we should come together in judgment. Neither is there any daysman (mediator) betwixt us, that might lay his hand upon us both" (Job 9:32, 33).

The union of the divine and the human natures in one person, theologically called "the hypostatical union" is the ground of perfect mediation.

4. The Son of God Became Incarnate To Provide the Sacrifice for Sin.

"If a man sin he shall bring an offering." "Without the shedding of blood there is no remission" (Heb. 9:22).

As sinners we needed a sacrifice for our sin and our sins. God's infinitely holy and righteous character and His government demanded, and that absolutely, inflexibly, and eternally, that your sin, and my sin, be duly and fully punished, for infinite justice must be met and satisfied as regards all sin.

Through sin, all were shut up to judgment. Guilty and unable to provide any offering that was acceptable in His sight, we were going to certain punishment, for we read, "And as it is appointed unto men once to die, but after this the judgment" (Heb. 9:27). Such was man's plight. If anything was to be done for him, God only could do it. The whole human family were condemned criminals and positively unable to atone for their crimes. A hopeless case! Yes, apart from God's gracious provision in Christ Jesus.

You remember the story recorded in the twenty-second chapter of Genesis. Abraham, in response to God's command, was on his way up the mountain when Isaac turned to his father and asked about the lamb for the burnt offering. Abraham answered, "My son, God will provide *himself* a lamb for the burnt offering" (Gen. 22:8). Thanks be unto Him! for when we had nothing to bring, He in infinite love and mercy provided the lamb for the burnt offering in the person of His own Son. "Behold the Lamb of God, which taketh away the sin of the world" (John 1:29). "Who his own self bare our sins in his own body on the tree, that we, being dead to sins, should live unto righteousness: by whose stripes we are healed" (I Pet. 2:24). "God sending his own Son in the likeness of sinful flesh, and for sin, condemned sin in the flesh" (Rom. 8:3).

Personally, I accepted that sacrifice for my sin and my sins more than thirty-eight years ago. That sacrifice is still efficacious and ever will be; therefore I need never seek for any other sacrifice and neither need you. Brother, believe it; sinner, receive it!

"By His immaculate sacrifice, the covenant is confirmed, its promises are sure to His spiritual seed, and there is no condemnation to those who believe in Him" (Dick).

"Neither by the blood of goats and calves, but by his own blood he entered in once into the holy place, having obtained eternal redemption for us. For if the blood of bulls and of goats, and the ashes of an heifer sprinkling the unclean, sanctifieth to the purifying of the flesh: how much more shall not the blood of Christ, who through the eternal Spirit offered himself without spot to God, purge your conscience from dead works to serve the living God?" (Heb. 9:12-14).

5. *Christ Came in the Likeness of Sinful Flesh To Be a Merciful and Faithful High Priest.* "Wherefore in all things it behooved him to be made like unto his brethren, that he might be a merciful and faithful high priest in things pertaining to God, to make reconciliation for the sins of the people" (Heb. 2:17).

The sinner needed the sacrifice for his sins; the believer needs the priest. Christ coming in the flesh supplied both needs: On the Cross He did everything necessary for the sinner's salvation; His great high priestly ministry as Intercessor and Advocate is for His own.

Concerning His high priestly ministry we read, "Who is he that condemneth? It is Christ that died, yea, rather, that is risen again, who is even at the right hand of God, who also maketh intercession for us" (Rom. 8:33). "Wherefore he is able also to save them to the uttermost that come unto God by him, seeing he ever liveth to make intercession for them" (Heb. 7:25).

"For Christ is not entered into the holy places made with hands, which are figures of the true; but into heaven itself, now to appear in the presence of God for us" (Heb. 9:24). "And if any man sin, we have an Advocate with the Father, Jesus Christ the righteous; and he is the propitiation for our sins; and not for ours only, but also for the whole world" (I John 2:2).

6. *The Son of God Became Incarnate To Destroy the Works of the Devil.* "For this purpose was the Son of God manifested that he might destroy the works of the devil" (I John 3:8). "Forasmuch then as the children are partakers of flesh and blood, he also himself likewise took part of the same; that through death he might destroy him that had the power of death, that is, the devil; and to deliver them who through fear of death were all their lifetime subject to bondage" (Heb. 2:14, 15).

In the Old Testament we read that he opened not the house of his prisoners (Isa. 14:17). Paul says, "And having spoiled (stripped or disarmed) principalities and powers, he made a shew of them openly, triumphing over them in it" (Col. 2:15).

7. *The Son of God Became Incarnate To Fulfil the Davidic Covenant.* "He shall be great, and shall be called the Son of the Highest: and the Lord God shall give unto him the throne of his father David: and he shall reign over the house of Jacob forever; and of his kingdom there shall be no end" (Luke 1:31, 32). In His glorified human body He will appear and reign as "KING OF KINGS AND LORD OF LORDS" (Rev. 19:16).

His right and title to the throne are absolutely established by the genealogies in Matthew and Luke. Had this not been absolutely certain, His bitterest enemies, the Pharisees, would have made use of the fact when they sought for something against Him.

In the Old Testament we read, "Of the increase of his government and peace there shall be no end, upon the throne of David, and upon his kingdom, to order it, and to establish it with judgment and with justice from henceforth even for ever. The zeal of the Lord of hosts will perform this" (Isa. 9:7). "Behold, the days come, saith the LORD, that I will raise unto David a righteous Branch, and a King shall reign and prosper, and shall execute judgment and justice in the earth" (Jer. 23:5).

8. *The Son of God Became Incarnate To Be the Head Over All Things to the Church.* "And hath put all things under his feet, and gave him to be the head over all things to the church, which is his body, the fulness of him that filleth all in all" (Eph. 1:22, 23).

The church is "the mystery which was kept secret since the world began" (Rom. 16:25). To the Apostle Paul was given the complete revelation concerning this mystery (Eph. 3:1-7).

The church, which is His body, is, as we will see later in our studies, the supreme product of the death, burial and resurrection of our Lord Jesus Christ.

The Word makes a distinction between the first principles of the teaching of Christ and the deep things of God. The first is concerning God's purpose in the earth—the Messianic Kingdom, the mediatorial reign of the Lord Jesus Christ upon the throne of His father David. The deep things of God are concerning God's purpose for heaven—the Church, the heavenly company, "the bringing of many sons unto glory."

CHAPTER IX.

THE VIRGIN BIRTH

Three Reasons Why the Virgin Birth of Christ Was Absolutely Necessary

1. *It Was Necessary in Order that Prophecy Might Be Fulfilled.*

Three Old Testament prophecies and one in the New Testament absolutely demand that the Messiah be born of a virgin. "The Scripture cannot be broken" (John 10:35).

In the Old Testament we are told, "And I will put enmity between thee and the woman, and between thy seed and her seed; it shall bruise thy head, and thou shalt bruise his heel" (Gen. 3:15).

This prophecy has always been interpreted to refer to Christ, who would finally overcome Satan, and then set up His kingdom on the earth. The word "seed" (Greek "sperma") when used in the Scriptures concerning human beings, always refers to the father and not the mother, with this one exception.

The Messiah must be both the son of David, and of the seed of David. The word "son" may express natural, or blood relationship, but it may also express merely legal relationship. Saul called David "my son," evidently on the ground that David was his son-in-law (I Sam. 24:16) and not a real son by blood. Joseph was a son of David; Christ was the legal son of Joseph and therefore the son of David. Since Mary was a direct descendant by blood from David (which a careful comparison of the genealogies of our Lord in Matthew and Luke will reveal), it is therefore evident that to be the seed of this woman was to be of the seed of David.

This is in keeping with the prophecy in Isaiah, "Behold, a virgin shall conceive, and bear a son, and shall call his name Immanuel" (Isa. 7:14). According to Matthew this prophecy was fulfilled by the birth of Jesus Christ (Matt. 1:22).

We also read, "For the LORD hath created a new thing in the earth, a woman shall compass a man" (Jer. 31:22). The virgin birth of our Lord was a new thing in the earth. It was something that had never before been, and has never since been repeated.

Being the legal son of Joseph, the husband of Mary, and of the seed of David on His mother's side these prophecies were fulfilled. This harmonizes with the New Testament prophecy, in which the angel said to Mary, "And, behold, thou shalt conceive in thy womb, and bring forth a son, and shalt call his name JESUS. The Holy Ghost shall come upon thee, and the power of the Highest shall overshadow thee: therefore also that holy thing which shall be born of thee shall be called the Son of God" (Luke 1:31, 35).

2. *The Virgin Birth of Christ Was Necessary that He Might Be Entitled to the Throne of His Father David.*

Through the prophet Jeremiah, God disclosed a bar and a ban upon the royal line of Judah. Jeremiah says, "Is this man Coniah (Jeconiah, Jehoiakin) a despised broken idol? Is he a vessel wherein is no pleasure? Wherefore are they cast out, he and his seed, and are cast into a land which they know not? O earth, earth, earth, hear the word of the LORD. Thus saith the LORD: Write ye this man childless, a man that shall not prosper in his days: for no man of his seed shall prosper, sitting upon the throne of David and ruling any more in Judah" (Jer. 22:28-30). Coniah was the last king in the royal succession to occupy the throne of David. He was not childless, for we are distinctly told that he had children. We read, "And the sons of Jeconiah; Assir, Salathiel his son" (I Chron. 3:17); "And after they were brought to Babylon, Jechonias begat Salathiel" (Matt. 1:12).

The title to the throne of David must descend through the line of Coniah. There was no other way. But note, that every natural descendant of this man was barred from the throne. In order that Christ might occupy the throne of His father David He must establish His legal right through the line that rested under the pronounced curse.

He must be a son of David through the male line of succession, so that He might occupy the throne of David, but in order that He might escape the curse pronounced upon that line, He must *not* be the seed of Coniah. Christ was the son of David and also of the seed of David. For in Matthew 1:16 we read, "Jacob begat Joseph, the husband of Mary, of whom was born Jesus, who is called the Christ." He was of the seed of David on his mother's side.

Joseph was the husband of Mary (married by divine direction) before the birth of Christ. This made Christ the legal son of Joseph, without being of the seed of Joseph—the son of David but not of the seed of Coniah.

Thus we see how Christ, being born of a virgin, met all demands of prophecy, and at the same time escaped all the bars of prophecy, thus securing an unmistakable title to the throne of His father David.

3. The Virgin Birth Was Necessary that We Might Have a Saviour.

In the first section of this book we have shown by the writings of the Apostle Paul that the whole human race sinned in Adam (Rom. 5:12; I Cor. 15:22). Adam was the federal head of the race; when he fell, the whole race fell in him.

Adam was also the natural head of the race; therefore every one descending from him by natural generation is a partaker of his fallen sinful nature (Rom. 5:19; Gen. 5:3).

This once and for all barred all the natural descendants of Adam from the work of redemption from sin, for we read, "None of them can by any means redeem his brother, nor give to God a ransom for him: For the redemption of their soul is precious, and it ceaseth forever" ("It must be left alone for ever")— (Psalm 49:7, 8), and so it had to be as far as mere man was concerned.

Therefore, if man was ever to be saved, some one had to come into the human race, who did not come under any of the various aspects of sin.

However, in order to be the sinner's substitute it was necessary for the Redeemer to be a real man, a kinsman; but to be an adequate substitute He had to be "holy, harmless, undefiled and separate from sinners." This our Lord would not have been had He been the natural son of Joseph. He had to be man in order that He might die as the sacrifice for sin; He had to be God in order that His death might be efficacious. Being born of the virgin Mary, it was possible for Christ to be our Saviour.

We have already noted that His virgin birth was predicted in the Old Testament, and that the words of the angel as recorded by Luke revealed how it would be accomplished. We read, "And the angel said unto her, The Holy Ghost shall come upon thee, and the power of the Highest shall overshadow thee: therefore also that holy thing which shall be born of thee shall be called the Son of God" (Luke 1:35).

Paul's statement, "God sending his own Son in the likeness of sinful flesh" (Rom. 8:3), clearly and positively teaches the pre-existence of our Lord, and His virgin birth. Note how carefully Paul guards his words in the statement. Had our Lord come in sinful flesh, He Himself would have been in need of a Saviour.

To the Galatians Paul writes, "But when the fulness of time was come, God sent forth his Son, made of a woman, made under the law, to redeem them that were under the law, that we might receive the adoption of sons" (Gal. 4:4, 5).

Concerning the body of our Lord we read, "Wherefore when he cometh into the world, he saith, Sacrifice and offering thou wouldest not, but a body hast thou prepared me" (Heb. 10:5). Our Lord's body was especially prepared for Him. The angel referred to Him as "that holy thing."

CHAPTER X.

THE ONE ACT OF OBEDIENCE

"For as by one man's disobedience many were made sinners, so by the obedience of one shall many be made righteous" (Rom. 5:19).

In Romans 5:18 the Apostle wrote about "the righteousness of one" and the result thereof. It is important to note that Paul does not say the many righteous acts. Every act of our Lord was infinitely righteous; yet one is singled out from among all the rest, and this one righteous act was the one that brought salvation to lost sinners.

Many say that it was not absolutely necessary for the Lord Jesus to die on the Cross; God could have saved lost sinners through some other means. Others claim that it was through His life of perfect obedience that we are saved. His infinitely perfect life does enter into our redemption for just as the Old Testament offerings had to be perfect both outwardly and inwardly, so Christ as our Sacrifice was the "Lamb without blemish and without spot" (I Peter 1:19).

Our Lord "knew no sin" (II Cor. 5:21), and He committed no sin; He was therefore the one and the only one that was qualified to suffer in the place of sinful men. In that aspect His life of perfect obedience does enter into our redemption from sin. But, and if, our Lord had lived on in the flesh in infinitely perfect obedience up to this very moment, we of the Gentiles

TWO MEN — TWO ACTS — TWO RESULTS
1 COR 15:45-50; ROM 5:12-21

PHIL 2:8
1 COR 15:3

ADAM
GEN 1:26-31
GEN 2:7-8
GEN 2:15-17
GEN 3:1-7
ROM 5:12

THE LAW
ROM 5:20
ROM 8:3
HEB 7:19

CHRIST
ROM 8:3
GAL 4:4-5
HEB 2:9

THE FALLEN RACE — GEN. 5:3 — EP

Four Aspects } IMPUTED   IN NATURE   IN
Of Sin   Rom. 5:12   Rom. 5:19   Ro

DESIGNED BY JAY

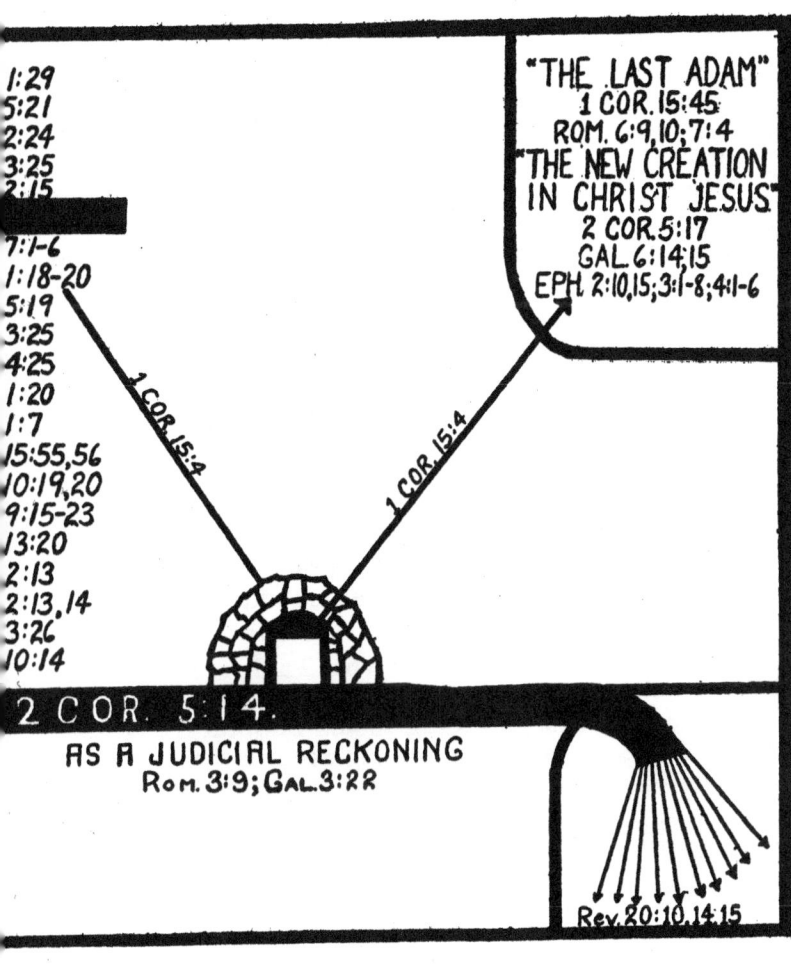

would still be without a Saviour. Concerning the Gentiles we are told, "That at that time ye were without Christ, being aliens from the commonwealth of Israel, strangers from the covenants of promise, having no hope, and without God in the world" (Eph. 2:12). We also read, "Christ has redeemed us from the curse of the law, being made a curse for us: for it is written, Cursed is every one that hangeth on a tree: that the blessing of Abraham might come to the Gentiles through Jesus Christ; that we might receive the promise of the Spirit through faith" (Gal. 3:13, 14).

These Scriptures reveal the absolute necessity of the death of Christ on the Cross, by the Apostle Paul designated as the supreme act of obedience on the part of our Lord. He writes, "And being found in fashion as a man, he humbled himself, and became obedient unto death, even the death of the cross" (Phil. 2:8).

Our Lord's obedience unto death is the one righteous act of the Second Man that reaches unto all unto justification of life, and is placed over against the one offence of the first man that reached unto all men unto condemnation.

This one righteous act is what Paul refers to when he defines the gospel that he preached—"that Christ died for our sins according to the Scriptures" (I Cor. 15:3). Apart from this one righteous act there is no gospel—no hope for guilty, lost, undone sinners.

Things Accomplished by the Death of Christ on the Cross.

Before looking into the things that the death of Christ on the cross accomplished, we shall briefly sum up what we have so far considered.

Sin, the most awful thing in the Universe, entered the world through Adam, the first man. His original sin is imputed to the race; every child of Adam is a partaker of his fallen nature and is therefore predisposed to sin. Sin so degrades man that he has no ability whatsoever to do that which is good in the sight of God. Man is not only a sinner, he is dead in trespasses and sins, and can produce nothing but sin.

The Law was given to Israel, but not as a cure or a remedy for man's fallen and lost estate. It was not given to justify, to save nor to make man good. In that respect it was and still is a total failure. The Law is good only when lawfully used, and we have seen from the Word what its true purpose is. The Law could not rescue man from his lost estate, because "it was weak through the flesh."

Christ, the Eternal Son of God, came into this world in "the likeness of sinful flesh." He became man, primarily that He might die; He was born for that very purpose. He was the Lamb provided by God the Father and as the Lamb of God went all the way to the Cross where He, the "Second Man," gave Himself as the sacrifice for the sin and the sins of the first man and his posterity. He had to become man in order that He might die but He had to be God in order that His death might be efficacious as the sacrifice for sin. The Cross was both the supreme manifestation of God's love and the supreme manifestation of sin.

And now, we are ready to look into the things His death once and for all accomplished. The Scriptures indicated on the Chart are but a few of the many that will be considered.

1. *On the Cross There Was a Dealing with Imputed Sin* — John 1:29 — "Behold, the Lamb of God, which taketh away the sin of the world."

The sin that entered through the first man and which was imputed to the rest of the race was taken away by the Second Man when He, as the Lamb of God, died on the Cross.

He was the burnt offering, which typifies Christ offering Himself without spot to God in pure delight to do His Father's will even unto death. His sacrifice was voluntary for He said, "No man taketh it (His life) from me, but I lay it down of myself. I have power to lay it down, and I have power to take it again. This commandment have I received of my Father" (John 10:18).

Through the sacrifice of Christ as the Lamb of God provided for sin, God was glorified concerning sin. This aspect of the death of Christ is the ground upon which the innocent child is saved. He dies because he is guilty in Adam, but is saved, not as some teach, on the ground of innocency, but because Christ as the Lamb of God took away the sin of the world.

2. *On the Cross There Was a Dealing with Sin in Nature*—II Cor. 5:21—"For he hath made him to be sin for us, who knew no sin; that we might be made the righteousness of God in him."

Here the reference is to the sin nature that every one possesses—what man is in Adam. It has in view Christ's death for sin, not sins. Christ did not descend by natural generation from Adam and so He was not involved in Adam's sin. He was "holy, harmless, undefiled and separate from sinners" (Heb. 7:26). On the Cross, He was made what we were that we might become or be what He is.

It is not said that Christ was made *a sinner* but that He was made sin. There is a vast difference between the two terms. God loves the sinner but He abhors sin. And yet His own and only beloved Son was made sin that we might become in Him the righteousness of God.

His death was a judgment upon every aspect of sin. Paul says, "God sending his own Son in the likeness of sinful flesh, and for sin, condemned sin in the flesh." (Rom. 8:3). The old sin nature was not only judged and condemned but it was also executed, for we are told that "our old man is (was) crucified with him" (Rom. 6:6). We were identified with Christ on the Cross; had we not been there, He never would have been there because He was the Sinless One. He had no sins to suffer for and was therefore deathless—beyond the reach of death.

We also read, "For the love of Christ constraineth us; because we thus judge, that if one died for all, then were all dead" (II Cor. 5:14). Paul uses the Greek aorist tense, so the last phrase should read, "then all died."

From these Scriptures we learn that our Lord's death on the Cross was for sin, but it was also unto sin. Sin, the old nature, is therefore judged, condemned and executed—judicially dead. And so, we, as believers through the Cross have been delivered from sin, the cruel master by whom we were held in bondage. "Likewise reckon ye also yourselves to be dead indeed unto sin, but alive unto God through Jesus Christ our Lord" (Rom. 6:11).

3. *On the Cross There Was a Dealing with Sin in Action*—I Peter 2:24—"Who his own self bare our sins in his own body on the tree, that we, being dead to sins, should live unto righteousness: by whose stripes ye were healed."

This refers to sins, sin in action. Sin is what we are in Adam, our sin nature; sins are the outworking of that nature and so what we ourselves do. Sin is the tree, sins, the fruit.

Christ, as the trespass offering in a very special

way, took care of sin in action. Note carefully that Peter says, "That we, being dead to sins." Paul tells us that our death with Christ was "unto sin." The believer is therefore dead unto sin and sins; the shackles of sin and sins are for ever broken. Being "dead to sins" does not mean that Christians can no longer sin, but it does mean just what Paul says when he writes, "Blessed is the man to whom the Lord will not impute sin" (Rom. 4:8). Here Paul speaks about the one that God has declared righteous through faith in Christ. "But to him that worketh not, but believeth on him that justifieth the ungodly, his faith is counted for righteousness" (Rom. 4:5).

One of the immediate results of Adam's original sin was that he acquired guilt. The whole race was condemned in him. Paul, in the Epistle to the Romans, in speaking of the full result of the Gospel of Grace, asks, "Who shall lay any thing to the charge of God's elect? It is God that justifieth" (Rom. 8:33). No, God will never reverse His verdict. The justified one is cleared of all guilt, past, present and future. The believer has entered into a new relationship with God. He is no longer dealt with as a judge deals with a criminal, but rather as a loving father deals with his child. He will chasten His sinning child, but never condemn him with the world, "For if we would judge ourselves, we should not be judged. But when we are judged, we are chastened of the Lord, that we should not be condemned with the world" (I Cor. 11:31, 32). The result of this judgment is stated in verse 30 where we read, "For this cause many are weak and sickly among you, and many sleep" (have died).

4. *On the Cross There Was a Final Dealing with Pre-Cross Sins*—Rom. 3:25—"Whom God hath set forth to be a propitiation through faith in his blood, to declare his righteousness for the remission (passing by)

of sins that are past, through the forbearance of God."

When Paul says God "passed by" sins, he does not imply that He in any way made light of sin, for God can not do that. The cross of Christ is a manifest token that this is impossible. On the cross there was a final dealing with the sins of the Old Testament saints. We are told, "And for this cause he is the mediator of the new testament (covenant), that by means of death, for the redemption of the transgressions that were under the first testament (covenant), they which are called might receive the promise of eternal inheritance" (Heb. 9:15).

Before the cross, animal sacrifices were offered to atone for (cover) their sins. But it was not possible for the blood of these sacrifices to take away sins; it only covered them. God forgave their sins on the ground of what was to be accomplished by Christ on the cross. There all sins that had been but covered before were completely blotted out. This is clearly revealed in the Scriptures. "For the life of the flesh is in the blood: and I have given it to you upon the altar to make an atonement for your souls: for it is the blood that maketh an atonement for your soul" (Lev. 17:11). The Hebrew word translated "atonement" means "covering." Theologically the word "atonement" has been used as the term covering the whole sacrificial and redemptive work of Christ. This is not altogether correct according to the Scriptures. Much more than "atonement" was accomplished by the cross of Christ. We read, "For it is not possible that the blood of bulls and of goats should take away sins" (Heb. 10:4); "And every priest standeth daily ministering and offering oftentimes the same sacrifices, which can never take away sins: But this man, after he had offered one sacrifice for sins for ever, sat down on the right hand of God" (Heb. 10:11, 12).

The legal sacrifices covered the offerer's sins and secured for him divine forgiveness. They were forgiven on credit; God, so to speak, gave them a promissory note. This was redeemed on the cross of Christ.

5. *On the Cross There Was a Spoiling Judgment upon Satan and the Powers of Evil*—Col. 2:15—"And having spoiled principalities and powers, he made a show of them openly, triumphing over them in it"— The Cross.

When the LORD God pronounced sentence upon Satan way back in the Garden, He said, "Because thou hast done this, thou art cursed above all cattle, and above every beast of the field; upon thy belly shalt thou go, and dust shalt thou eat all the days of thy life: And I will put enmity between thee and the woman, and between thy seed and her seed; it shall bruise thy head, and thou shalt bruise his heel" (Gen. 3:14, 15).

For centuries Satan has ruled the world (kosmos) as a usurper without right and title. He is still the "prince of this world" (John 14:30); and "the god of this age" (II Cor. 4:4). Before the cross he had a strangle hold on the Gentiles since they had no way of approach to God whatsoever. Christ was manifested that He might destroy the works of the devil (I John 3:8). This was accomplished on the cross. Our Lord referred to it when He said, "Now is the judgment of this world: now shall the prince of this world be cast out" (John 12:31), and, "Of judgment, because the prince of this world is judged" (John 16:11). "Forasmuch then as the children are partakers of flesh and blood, he also himself likewise took part of the same; that through death he might destroy him that had the power of death, that is, the devil" (Heb. 2:14).

On the cross Satan was stripped or disarmed of

the power of death. He is defeated, a conquered enemy, and under the sentence of death. In God's own time he will be cast into the lake of fire, the place especially prepared for him and his angels (Matt. 25:41; Rev. 20:10). For we read, "And the devil that deceived them was cast into the lake of fire and brimstone, where are the beast and the false prophet, and shall be tormented day and night for ever and ever" (Rev. 20:10).

6. *On the Cross the Law Came to an End*—Rom. 7:1-6—"Know ye not, brethren, for I speak to them that know the law, how that the law hath dominion over a man as long as he liveth? For the woman which hath an husband is bound by the law to her husband so long as he liveth; but if the husband be dead, she is loosed from the law of her husband. So then if, while her husband liveth, she be married to another man, she shall be called an adulteress: but if her husband be dead, she is free from that law; so that she is no adulteress, though she be married to another man. Wherefore, my brethren, ye also are become dead to the law by the body of Christ; that ye should be married to another, even to him who is raised from the dead, that we should bring forth fruit unto God. For when we were in the flesh, the motions of sins, which were by the law, did work in our members to bring forth fruit unto death. But now we are delivered from the law, that being dead wherein we were held; that we should serve in newness of spirit, and not in the oldness of the letter."

"For Christ is the end of the law for righteousness to every one that believeth" (Rom. 10:4).

The Law was not given as a permanent institution; for we read, "It was added because of transgressions, till the seed should come to whom the promise was made" (Gal. 3:19).

This plainly teaches that the Law is done away with for that person who exercises saving faith. This does not mean to merely quit sinning in action, for if every unsaved person would cease sinning and never commit another sin as long as they lived, that would not make one more Christian. For, if one who has broken the Law suddenly begins to keep it, that does not take care of the Law that has already been broken. The Law is not established until the full penalty of the broken Law is paid in full. Christ established the Law by paying the penalty of the Law and that to an infinite degree.

When a sinner exercises saving faith—ceases from his own work and trusts in Christ for salvation—he is justified, declared righteous, and we are told that "Law is not made for a righteous man, but for the lawless and disobedient, for the ungodly and for sinners, for unholy and profane, for murderers of fathers and murderers of mothers, for manslayers, for whoremongers, for them that defile themselves with mankind, for menstealers, for liars, for perjured persons, and if there be any other thing that is contrary to sound doctrine" (I Tim. 1:9, 10).

Paul calls the Law "the ministration of death." It was given to Israel and was the means by which the old creation was slain. Paul says, "For I through the law am dead to the law, that I might live unto God" (Gal. 2:19).

Sin and the Law are inseparably linked together in the Scriptures. When the Law killed the old man it drove him out of its realm, beyond its reach. "For he that is dead is freed from sin" (Rom. 6:7).

The Scriptures clearly teach that the Law is done away with both as the means of justification and as the rule of life and conduct for the one who through faith in Christ has been justified from all things, "Wherefore the law was our schoolmaster to bring us unto Christ, that we might be justified by faith. But after that faith is come, we are no longer under a schoolmaster" (Gal. 3:24, 25).

The believer is not under the Law, but under grace. Concerning this Paul says, "For sin shall not have dominion over you: for ye are not under the law, but under grace" (Rom. 6:14). The grace rule of life is the heavenly standard; it warrants a heavenly walk of a heavenly people right here on earth.

Before the cross the Mosaic Law was the divine rule of life for God's earthly people. The Kingdom Law will be the rule of life during the Millennium. Between the two legal rules of life stands the heavenly, a rule of pure grace.

The moral and spiritual values of the Law are carried over into the teachings of grace, but always and absolutely without the meritorious feature. All but one (the fourth) of the Ten Commandments reappear under grace, but without the meritorious feature.

Between the Word of God and modern theology there is an absolute contradiction with reference to the Law. Modern theology says we are under the Law as a rule of life. The Word of God says, "But after faith is come, we are no longer under the schoolmaster" (Gal. 3:25). With which do you agree?

While it is true that the Law by means of death drove the sinner out of its realm and beyond its reach, there are many who today are under the Law. Who are they? and why are they there? Many say the Jews, to whom the Law was given, are still under the Law. Others believe the unsaved are under the Law. Neither answer is correct. Before the cross Israel was under the Law, and as God's covenant people enjoyed all the privileges and blessings. There was between the Circumcision and the Uncircumcision a vast difference positionally (not morally). Concerning Israel Paul writes, "Who are Israelites; to whom pertaineth the adoption, and the glory, and the covenants, and the giving of the law, and the service of God, and the promises; whose are the fathers, and of whom as concerning the flesh Christ came, who is over all, God blessed for ever. Amen" (Rom. 9:4, 5). Concerning the Gentiles he says, "That at that time ye were without Christ, being aliens from the commonwealth of Israel, and strangers from the covenants of promise, having no hope, and without God in the world" (Eph. 2:12).

The cross completely eliminated this difference; not by bringing the Gentiles *up* to the level of the Jews, but rather by bringing the Jews *down* to the level of the Gentiles. They are all "under sin" (Rom. 3:9) and judicially dead (II Cor. 5:14). All must come to God through faith in Christ. Paul says, "But the scripture hath concluded all under sin, that the promise by faith of Jesus Christ might come to them that believe" (Gal. 3:22).

Neither are the unsaved under the Law. There is no rule of life for a dead person. The issue between God and the unsaved is not how they are to behave themselves, but what they do with Christ. Preaching a rule of life to the unsaved is as unreasonable as going into a mortuary and telling the lifeless bodies that may be there, how to conduct themselves. No, the message to the lost is the Gospel of God's grace, which reveals to lost and undone sinners how they may obtain life.

It is the one who voluntarily places himself on legal ground by trusting in his works to justify or to keep himself justified and so complements grace that is under the Law. We read, "For I testify again to every man that is circumcised, that he is a debtor to do the whole law" (Gal. 5:3).

It is just as much out of place for a Christian to put himself under the Law, and so be under the Law and grace at the same time, as it is for a woman to have two husbands. There are many who are guilty of spiritual polyandry.

To apply the "by works" principle to the unsaved is to be guilty of preaching "another gospel"; and to apply the same principle to the saved is to encourage them to "fall from grace."

The cross brings to an end all that man is, and all that he can be or do by nature. It ends his life and reckons him dead before God; a dead man, whose death was the death of one guilty of the greatest crime in the Universe. To impose the Law upon the one that God has declared righteous in Christ is but to resurrect the criminal. "Do we then make void the law through faith? God forbid: yea, we establish the law" (Rom. 3:31).

7. *On the Cross the Work of Redemption Was Once and For All Accomplished*—I Peter 1:18-20— "Forasmuch as ye know that ye were not redeemed with corruptible things, as silver and gold, from your vain conversation received by tradition from your fathers; but with the precious blood of Christ, as of a lamb without blemish and without spot: Who verily was foreordained before the foundation of the world, but was manifested in these last times for you."

To redeem means to loose, to set free or deliver by paying a price. Man is "sold under sin" (Rom. 7:14); he is under the sentence of death (Ezek. 18:4).

Redemption is by blood and by power. It is wholly of God both in type and antitype. When the Lord called Moses He said, "I have surely seen the affliction of my people which are in Egypt, and have heard their cry by reason of their taskmasters; for I know their sorrows; and I am come down to deliver them out of the hand of the Egyptians, and to bring them up out of that land unto a good land and a large, unto a land flowing with milk and honey" (Exodus 3:7, 8). "For God so loved the world, that he gave his only begotten Son, that whosoever believeth in him should not perish, but have everlasting life." Note that God said "I am come down," and that it was He who loved, and gave His all for our redemption.

Redemption is through a person, and this person must be a kinsman of the one that is to be redeemed. We read, "If thy brother be waxed poor, and hath sold away some of his possessions, and if any of his kin come to redeem it, then shall he redeem that which his brother sold" (Lev. 25:25). "After that he is sold he may be redeemed again; one of his brethren may redeem him; either his uncle, or his uncle's son, may redeem him, or any that is nigh of kin unto him of his family may redeem him; or if he be able, he may redeem himself" (Lev. 25:48, 49).

But in order that he be able to redeem, the kinsman must not in any way be involved himself. Christ our Redeemer met this requirement for He was "holy, harmless, undefiled and separate from sinners." A redeemer must also be willing to redeem. Our Lord said, "No man taketh it from me, but I lay it down of myself" (John 10:18).

The redemptive work of Christ includes the redemption of the body (Rom. 8:23); the whole creation (Rom. 8:21); the kingdoms of this world (Dan. 2:44, 45; Rev. 11:15); and the heavenly realm (Rev. 12:7-12).

8. *On the Cross the Work of Reconciliation Was*

Accomplished—II Cor. 5:19—"To-wit, that God was in Christ, reconciling the world unto himself, not imputing their trespasses unto them; and hath committed unto us the word of reconciliation."

Reconcile means "to change thoroughly from." It is accomplished by removing the cause of disagreement or disharmony. It is to restore peaceful relations between two persons at variance. In the business world the word reconcile is often used with reference to the balancing of accounts.

As redemption is toward sin, so reconciliation refers to the effect of the death of Christ upon man.

It was accomplished on the Cross ("And you, that were sometime alienated and enemies in your mind by wicked works, yet now hath he reconciled in the body of his flesh through death, to present you holy and unblameable and unreproveable in his sight" Col. 1:21-22) and it was while man was yet an enemy ("For if, when we were enemies, we were reconciled to God by the death of his Son, much more, being reconciled, we shall be saved by his life," Rom. 5:10).

In his letter to the Colossians Paul says, "For it pleased the Father that in him should all fulness dwell; and, having made peace through the blood of his cross, by him to reconcile all things unto himself; by him, I say, whether they be things in earth, or things in heaven" (Col. 1:20).

"The things on the earth" refers to man. This is clear from other portions of Scripture. "The things in the heavens" is by some taken to refer to the fallen angels. One statement of Scripture, however, excludes this view. We read, "For verily he took not on him the nature of angels; but he took on him the seed of Abraham" (Heb. 2:16). In order that He might become the author of eternal salvation, we are told that, "in all things it behooved him to be made like unto his brethren, that he might be a merciful and faithful high priest in things pertaining to God, to make reconciliation (propitiation) for the sins of his people" (Heb. 2:17).

The true meaning of the words of these two verses we understand to be that the Son of God interposed for the deliverance of men, and not of angels. He became man in order to provide salvation for men; He did not become an angel in order to save the angels.

If not the angels, what then in the heavens could be the object of His work of reconciliation? May we not in this statement see that there was through the death of Christ a reconciliation between the attributes of God? His holiness demanded, and that eternally and inflexibly, that the guilty sinner be punished for his crime. His love yearned to save and to bless the sinner.

The cross of Christ removed every obstacle, so that God is now infinitely free to do everything He desires for both the sinner and the saint.

9. *On the Cross the Work of Propitiation was Accomplished*—Rom. 3:25—"Whom God hath set forth a propitiation through faith in his blood, to declare his righteousness for the remission of sins that are past, through the forbearance of God."

"Wherefore in all things it behooved him to be made like unto his brethren, that he might be a merciful and faithful high priest in things pertaining to God, to make reconciliation (propitiation) for the sins of the people" (Heb. 2:17).

Christ, by means of His death, made propitiation; He also is our propitiation. This work of His tells of the effect of His death upon God. God is now propitious toward the sinner. He could not save the sinner apart from blood. In the Old Testament, only the sprinkling of blood on the Ark of the Covenant could change it from a seat of judgment to a mercy seat. So the shed blood of Christ provides a righteous basis upon which an infinitely holy God can meet and commune with sinful man. In Hebrews 9:5 we read, "And over it the cherubims of glory shadowing the mercy seat; of which we cannot now speak particularly."

This is one of God's marvelous provisions for our salvation and safekeeping. We are told, "Herein is love, not that we have loved God, but that he loved us, and sent his Son to be the propitiation for our sins" (I John 4:10); "And if any man sin, we have an Advocate with the Father. Jesus Christ the righteous: and he is the propitiation for our sins: and not for ours only, but also for the sins of the whole world" (I John 2:1, 2).

In and through the Cross of Christ God's holiness was vindicated rather than His wrath appeased.

10. *On the Cross the Ground of the Sinner's Justification Was Accomplished*—Rom. 4:25—"Who was delivered for (because of) our offences, and was raised again for (because of) our justification."

Had He not been delivered up because of our offences we would have had to be delivered up because of them. If this is not substitution, words do no longer have any meaning. The words, "He was raised again because of our justification" mean that the ground of our justification was accomplished by His vicarious death. The ground of our justification was accomplished once and for all, because then every obstacle was for ever removed and every condemnation that had come upon man because of sin, was perfectly and righteously taken care of. Every demand of infinite justice had been met.

Justification is a judicial term. It is the act of

declaring righteous. A judgment will result either in condemnation or justification. God's judgment upon sin could result in nothing but condemnation. Concerning this we read, "God sending his own Son in the likeness of sinful flesh, and for sin, condemned sin in the flesh" (Rom. 8:3). But when the sinner with the heart believes unto righteousness, he is justified, declared righteous in Christ, and is clothed with a robe of righteousness that is infinitely perfect. Concerning the redemptive work of Christ as the ground of the sinner's justification, Paul writes, "Being justified freely (without cause) by his grace through the redemption that is in Christ Jesus" (Rom. 3:24).

Justification is not progressive nor is it something one receives in portions. A child of God is no more justified after years of devoted service than he was the day he was saved. It is not something that takes place in the nervous system nor in the emotional nature of the individual, but rather something that takes place in the mind and reckoning of God.

11. *On the Cross Peace Was Made*—Col. 1:19, 20 —"For it pleased the Father that in him should all fulness dwell; And having made peace through the blood of his cross."

Peace is the logical result of reconciliation, the enmity having been removed. Sinners are often called upon to make their peace with God. This has already been accomplished once and for all on the cross— "Having made peace through the blood of his cross."

We are told that, "He is our peace" (Eph. 2:14) and that "He came and preached peace" (Eph. 2:17). "Therefore being justified by faith, we have peace with God through our Lord Jesus Christ" (Rom. 5:1).

In his letters to the Colossians and to the Philippians Paul speaks of the "peace of God." This is not the same as the "peace with God" that we have through our Lord Jesus Christ. All that have been justified have peace with God. But it is not true that all that have peace with God enjoy the peace of God. It is in the measure that we come to know God as our Father that we will experience the peace of God. Note carefully the context of the words of our Lord, "Come unto me all ye that labour and are heavy laden, and I will give you rest" (Matt. 11:28). It is the Lord Jesus who makes God known as Father, and that knowledge produces rest of soul.

Note what the peace of God does for the one who has learned to bring everything to Him. "Be careful for nothing; but in every thing by prayer and supplication with thanksgiving let your requests be made known unto God. And the peace of God, which passeth all understanding, shall keep your hearts and minds through Christ Jesus" (Phil. 4:6, 7). It will safeguard the heart and mind of the believer just as an army will garrison a city that is the objective of an enemy. Wonderful provision that has been made for all sinners saved by grace!

12. *On the Cross the Means of Perpetual Cleansing Was Provided*—I John 1:7 — "But if we walk in the light, as he is in the light, we have fellowship one with another, and the blood of Jesus Christ his Son cleanseth us from all sin."

This is addressed to the Children of God, and it speaks of the need of perpetual cleansing. Sin is not reckoned as guilt to the one that God has declared righteous in Christ, but it does defile the justified one. God cannot have fellowship with a defiled child of His, but He can and will cleanse, upon one condition, which is "if we walk in the light."

Walking in the light will reveal that we have sin.

The one who says he has no sin is deceived. The full revelation concerning walking in the light is given to us by John when he writes, "If we say that we have no sin, we deceive ourselves, and the truth is not in us. If we confess our sins, he is faithful and just to forgive us our sins, and to cleanse us from all unrighteousness. If we say that we have not sinned, we make him a liar, and his word is not in us" (I John 1:8-10).

We repeat, that walking in the light will reveal that we are still possessors of a sin nature, and that we have therefore sinned. This will be followed by honest confession, and upon that one condition God forgives and cleanses.

In the Old Testament this aspect of the work of Christ is typified by the sacrifice of the red heifer (Num. 19:1-22). The ashes of the burned animal were mixed with water and sprinkled on the people as a means of ceremonial cleansing. Ashes speak of a finished redemption, applied in water—the Word of God.

13. *On the Cross the Sting of Death Was Removed* —I Cor. 15:55, 56—"O death, where is thy sting? O grave, where is thy victory? The sting of death is sin; and the strength of sin is the law."

These verses speak of another blessed accomplishment of the cross. Christ bore the sting of death; it is therefore for ever gone for the believer. If the Lord tarries, death will overtake us, but the death and resurrection of our Lord have forever removed its sting.

Many years ago I had a painful experience. Now as I look back upon it I find it serves to illustrate this particular truth.

It happened on a beautiful summer day at a Sunday School picnic in western Washington. I was walking along with a friend when suddenly something hit me on the top of my head. I reached up to remove it and found a bee. Immediately, I released it. My friend remarked, "Well—that bee will never sting again."

"Why not?" I wanted to know.

"Because its sting is gone," he replied.

"But where is it?"

"It's in your head," he answered—and that was not difficult for me to believe.

Just so, though death may overtake us, the sting of death is for ever gone, for the believer, because Christ bore it on the cross.

No wonder the Apostle Paul speaks about death as he does when he says, "For I am now ready to be offered, and the time of my departure is at hand" (II Tim. 4:6).

The Greek word translated "departure" is a nautical word, which refers to spreading the sails, weighing the anchor and sailing out into the wide open sea. That is the way Paul looked upon death. He did not think of contraction but rather expansion, and that of the most wonderful kind.

This same thought is found in his letter to the Corinthians, where he says, "For we know that if our earthly house of this tabernacle were dissolved we have a building of God, an house not made with hands, eternal in the heavens" (II Cor. 5:1).

Death holds no fear for the believer, for when his time on earth is over, he will enter into a far better realm with the precious promise that one day his body will be raised again and be glorified, and so be with the Lord for ever.

14. *On the Cross a New and Living Way Was Consecrated*—Heb. 10:19, 20—"Having therefore, brethren,

boldness to enter into the holiest by the blood of Jesus, by a new and living way, which he hath consecrated for us, through the veil, that is to say, his flesh."

In the Tabernacle the veil separated the holiest from the holy place and the outer court. The high priest only could enter within the veil, but not without blood.

When our Lord died on the Cross the veil in the temple was rent in twain from the top to the bottom. This signifies that a "new and living way" is open for all believers into the very presence of God through Christ our High Priest and Mediator. Apart from Him we have no access to God, for it is through the shed blood of Christ that the way is open and consecrated for us. We read, "And having a high priest over the house of God; let us draw near with a true heart in full assurance of faith, having our hearts sprinkled from an evil conscience, and our bodies washed with pure water" (Heb. 10:21, 22).

What a wonderful privilege it is, that we, unworthy as we are, can come into the presence of an infinitely holy and righteous God, and that we can so come with boldness.

15. *On the Cross the New Covenant Was Confirmed*—Heb. 9:15-17—"And for this cause he is the mediator of a new testament (covenant), that by means of death, for the redemption of the transgressions under the first testament (covenant), they which are called might receive the promise of eternal inheritance. For where a testament is, there must also of necessity be the death of the testator. For where a testament (covenant) is of force after men are dead: otherwise it is of no strength at all while the testator liveth."

Here the apostle compares and contrasts the new covenant with the old, the Mosaic. The Mosaic covenant was sealed with the blood of the animal sacrifices. The New Covenant was sealed and confirmed with the blood of Christ. He said, "For this is my blood of the new testament (covenant), which is shed for the remission of sins" (Matt. 26:28). The Mosaic covenant was made with Israel and, according to the plainest of teaching in the Old Testament and in the New, the New Covenant was to be made with the same people. In the Old Testament we read, "Behold, the days come, saith the LORD, that I will make a new covenant with the house of Israel, and with the house of Judah: not according to the covenant that I made with their fathers in the day I took them by the hand to bring them out of the land of Egypt; which covenant they brake, although I was an husband unto them, saith the LORD: But this shall be the covenant that I will make with the house of Israel; After those days, saith the LORD, I will put my law in their hearts; and will be their God, and they will be my people. And they shall teach no more every man his neighbour, and every man his brother, saying, Know the LORD: for they shall all know me, from the least of them unto the greatest of them, saith the LORD: for I will forgive their iniquity, and will remember their sin no more" (Jer. 31:31-34).

During the Kingdom Age, God's earthly people will be under the New Covenant, and enjoy its blessings. God never made any covenant with the Gentiles for they were "strangers to the covenants of promise" (Eph. 2:12).

The child of God is not related to Him on the basis of any covenant that He has made with man; he is related to Him by birth. Believers are born again, not of corruptible seed, but incorruptible, by the word of God, which liveth and abideth for ever" (I Peter 1:23).

Have we then no part in God's blessings? Of course we have, but they are secured for us under another covenant, of which we will now speak.

16. On the Cross the Covenant of Redemption Was Confirmed—Heb. 13:20—"Now the God of peace, that brought again from the dead our Lord Jesus, that great Shepherd of the sheep, through the blood of the everlasting (eternal) covenant."

Are not "everlasting" and "eternal" identical in meaning? No, something may begin today and go on for ever—that is everlasting. But that which is eternal in the true and full sense of the word is something that always was and always will be. It is from eternity to eternity. But, some one will say, "I received eternal life at such and such a time." Yes, indeed, but remember, the life you received when you were saved was the life of our Lord, who is before all time. When you with the heart believed unto righteousness you were by the Holy Spirit joined to the Lord. His life became your life, just as when a tender shoot is grafted on to a tree. If the operation is successful, the young branch will become a part of the tree; it will take part of the life of the tree that is past, that which is present, and also that which is future. Our Lord said, "At that day ye shall know that I am in my Father, and ye in me, and I in you" (John 14:20).

The death of Christ was the confirmation of the eternal covenant. This covenant is sometimes called the "Covenant of Redemption" and is referred to as the "Before all time Covenant." It is the covenant that Paul speaks of when he writes, "Brethren, I speak after the manner of men; though it be but a man's covenant, yet if it be confirmed, no man disannulleth, or addeth thereto. Now to Abraham and his seed were the promises made. He saith not, And to seeds, as of many; but as of one, And to thy seed, which is Christ. And this I say, that the covenant, that was confirmed before of God in Christ, the law, which was four hundred and thirty years after, cannot disannul, that it should make the promise of none effect" (Gal. 3:15-17).

This covenant was not made between God and man, but between the Persons of the Godhead, and it is concerning the salvation of man. It is now in force and has been ever since Christ's death on the cross. This covenant secures for ever for the believer "every spiritual blessing in the heavenly places in Christ." It provides far more and greater blessing than the Mosaic Covenant provided for God's earthly people before the cross, and also far greater blessings than the New Covenant has in store for God's earthly people in the yet future Kingdom Age.

17. *On the Cross Those Who Were Afar Off Were Made Nigh*—Eph. 2:13—"But now in Christ Jesus ye who sometimes were afar off are made nigh by the blood of Christ."

When Paul says, "ye who once were afar off," he refers primarily to the pre-cross position of the Gentiles? They are said to have been "afar off" (Eph. 2:17) as compared with the Jews. But there is a vast difference between the nigh position of the Jews as God's covenant people, and the nigh position of the one who today is "in Christ."

Through the animal sacrifices and the whole sacrificial system of Judaism, the covenant people had access to God, but the Gentiles had no way of approach to Him.

Note also, that we have been "made nigh by the blood of Christ." No works of our own, however good they may have been, could bring us nigh to God.

This is one of the exalted positions into which every believer is brought when he is saved. He is then made as nigh as he ever will be in time or eternity. But just how nigh are we? We are in Christ, members of His body, and therefore just as nigh to God as Christ, His own and only beloved Son, is. Oh, but we are not worthy of such an exalted position! No, praise God, He deals with us according to His mercy and grace and not our merits.

When James writes, "Draw nigh unto God, and he will draw nigh unto you" (James 4:9), he refers to the experimental aspect of nighness. Every position of the one that is in Christ has its corresponding experience in life. This is what James refers to.

18. *The Death of Christ Released the Blessing of Abraham*—Gal. 3:13, 14—"Christ hath redeemed from the curse of the law, being made a curse for us: for it is written, Cursed is every one that hangeth on a tree: That the blessing of Abraham might come to the Gentiles through Jesus Christ; that we might receive the promise of the Spirit through faith."

The blessing promised to Abraham is, "And in thee shall all the families of the earth be blessed" (Gen. 12:3); "the promise of the Spirit" is a reference to the words of Joel when he says, "And it shall come to pass afterward, that I will pour out my Spirit upon all flesh" (Joel 2:28).

The finished work of Christ—His death, burial and resurrection—opened the floodgates of divine love and grace to the Gentiles. He loved the Gentiles before, but the cross removed the hindrances which prevented the exercising of His love toward them, so making it possible for the blessing promised to Abraham to flow to them. God could not save them apart from blood.

"Without the shedding of blood there is no remission" (Heb. 9:22).

God is said to stretch out His arms ready to receive all who come to Him by Jesus Christ. No one needs to beg God to save him. Too often this legalistic feature has been imposed upon the unsaved. God is not unwilling to save sinners. "But," says some one, "I was saved when I prayed and asked God to be merciful to me." Yes, many have been saved when they prayed, but it was not because of their prayers they were saved. Many have prayed and did not get saved. The writer is one of them. A lost sinner is saved when he with the heart believes unto righteousness? The sinner is justified by faith, and the sinning child of God is forgiven and cleansed when he confesses his sin. The Apostle John writes to "my little children" when he says, "If we confess our sins, he is faithful and just to forgive us our sins, and to cleanse us from all unrighteousness" (I John 1:9).

19. *On the Cross It Was Made Possible for God To Exercise Absolute Justice and Mercy at the Same Time*—Rom. 3:26—"To declare, I say, at this time his righteousness: that he might be just, and the justifier of him which believeth in Jesus."

In this verse is revealed the solution of one of the greatest problems, if not the greatest, that infinite wisdom has solved. How could an infinitely holy and righteous God declare a guilty, vile sinner righteous and yet remain just?

Justification is a court matter and has to do with the relation of the accused one to the law. If someone has violated the law and is brought into court to answer the charges preferred against him, the judge that tries the case cannot exercise justice and mercy at the same time. If the violator of the law is sentenced to pay the full penalty of the broken law, there is no mercy. If the judge is lenient with the guilty one, and "lets him off easy," he does not exercise justice. It is not what the judge feels or thinks, but what the law says. The law is established when the penalty of the broken law is paid in full, and not until then. Christ on the cross endured the full penalty of the broken Law, when He once and for all met every demand of infinite holiness against sinners. It was on the cross that the broken Law was established.

Many years ago in a western court, a son of the judge was brought into court on a charge preferred against him. There father and son faced each other— the father on the bench as the judge and his own child before him as the accused one. The boy pleaded guilty and was by his father sentenced to pay the full penalty of the law. That was justice. But no sooner had the father pronounced sentence upon his child, than he stepped down from the bench and paid the fine he had sentenced him to pay. That was mercy. So today, because the Lord Jesus Christ, as the substitute for sinners, died in our room and in our stead, "the just for the unjust that he might bring us to God" (I Peter 3:18); every charge has been met, and God is infinitely free to do anything He desires for both sinner and saint. Every act of God in connection with our salvation is an act of infinite justice made possible by the cross of Christ.

20. *On the Cross the Sanctified Were Forever Perfected*—Heb. 10:14—"For by one offering hath he perfected for ever them that are sanctified."

This is in sharp contrast with the result of the animal sacrifices of the Old Testament economy, which merely covered sin for the time being. His precious blood shed upon the cross will never lose its efficacy. This perfection refers to the believer's position in Christ.

All these things that we have considered were accomplished once and for all when our Lord died on the cross. They represent what God has done for our salvation. Through them every obstacle has been removed. Through the death, burial and resurrection of Christ, man has been brought into a new position before God—not a saved, but a savable one. Jew and Gentile alike "are under sin." All merit is excluded. Every condemnation which divine righteousness could impose because of sin, and every human obligation has been disposed of. Every work of man has been set aside, and salvation is now offered to the guiltiest of sinners, as a gift of God's grace and upon the one condition of saving faith, which is to cease from one's own works and rest one's all in the finished work of Christ on the Cross.

Saving faith deposits One's eternal welfare and destiny into the grace of God. This is a definite act of the heart (the power to reason), "For with the heart man believeth unto righteousness" (Rom. 10:10). Have you so with the heart believed and received the gift of eternal life?

When salvation is made to depend on anything else than believing, the Scriptures are violated and the whole plan of salvation by grace is confused and made of none effect. Believing is the opposite of doing something in order to be saved. The Gospel of grace does not teach that the sinner must "believe and be baptized," "believe and pray," "believe and make restitution," "believe and repent," or "believe and confess." No, the sinner is saved by grace through faith *plus nothing*. To impose the principle of works as a condition for salvation is to place the individual on legal ground. Remember the words of Paul, "But to him that worketh not, but believeth on him that justifieth the ungodly, his faith is counted for righteousness" (Rom. 4:5). "There remaineth therefore a rest to the people of God. For he that hath entered into his rest, he also hath ceased from his own works, as God did from his" (Heb. 4:9, 10).

CHAPTER XI.

CHRIST'S BURIAL AND RESURRECTION
"He Was Buried"

In the first epistle to the Corinthians, Paul gives us the definition of the Gospel that he preached. He says, "For I delivered unto you first of all that which I also received, how that Christ died for our sins according to the scriptures; and that he was buried, and that he rose again the third day according to the scriptures" (I Cor. 15:3, 4).

Here we must make a distinction between the condescension of our Lord and His humiliation. When the Son of God, the Lord of Glory, came to this earth in the likeness of sinful flesh, it was condescension on His part; when He, on the Cross, was made a curse for us, and finally His body was placed in the tomb, He had reached the lowest depths of humiliation.

"Our Redeemer stooped low indeed when He assumed our nature, but lower still when He submitted to be laid in the grave. This is the last degree of humiliation. All the glory of man is extinguished in the tomb. If we viewed his prosperity with an eye of indifference, we now pity him; if his splendor excited our envy, the feeling dies away and hostility relents, when he, who like a flourishing tree spreads his branches around, now lies prostrate in the dust? Who is this that occupies the sepulchre of Joseph? Is it a prophet or a king? No; it is one greater than all prophets and kings, the Son of the living God, the Lord of heaven and earth; but there is now nothing to distinguish Him from the meanest of the human race; the tongue which charmed thousands with its eloquence is mute, and the hand which controlled the powers of the visible and invisible world is unnerved. The shades of death have enveloped Him, and silence reigns in His lonely abode." (Dick)

Not only was His body placed in the tomb, but He also descended into Hades. "Now that he ascended, what is it but that he also descended first into the lower parts of the earth?" (Eph. 4:9).

The significance of our Lord's burial was typified by the scape goat, upon whose head the high priest laid his hands and confessed the sins of the people, thereby transferring their sins to the animal that afterwards was sent away into the wilderness. Concerning this we read, "And when he hath made an end of reconciling (making atonement) the holy place, and the tabernacle of the congregation, and the altar, he shall bring in the live goat: And Aaron shall lay both his hands upon the head of the live goat, and confess over him all the iniquities of the children of Israel, and all their transgressions in all their sins, putting them upon the head of the goat, and shall send him away by the hand of a fit man into the wilderness: And the goat shall bear upon him all their iniquities unto a land not inhabited: and he shall let go the goat in the wilderness" (Lev. 16:20-22).

In the chorus of one of our great gospel hymns the truth is stated when we sing, "Living, He loved me; Dying, He saved me; *Buried; He carried my sins far away;* Rising, He justified freely forever; One day He's coming—oh, glorious day."

The humiliation of Christ manifests the greatness of His love and the riches of His grace, "For ye know the grace of our Lord Jesus Christ, that, though he was rich, yet for your sakes he became poor, that ye through his poverty might be rich" (II Cor. 8:9).

It was for us, men, and for our salvation, that He became man, and abased Himself to the dust of the earth. He drew a veil over His glory, that He might remove our reproach. He groaned and died that we might be redeemed and rescued from our lost estate, and that He might one day take us to be with Himself.

Let us learn humility from His example. Pride should forever be renounced by those who are His. He says, "Learn of me, for I am meek and lowly in heart, and ye shall find rest unto your souls" (Matt. 11:29). Paul writes, "Let this mind be in you, which was also in Christ Jesus: Who being in the form of God, thought it not robbery to be equal with God: But made himself of no reputation, and took upon him the form of a servant, and was made in the likeness of men: And being found in fashion as a man, he humbled himself, and became obedient unto death, even the death of the cross" (Phil. 2:5-8).

"He Rose Again the Third Day"

It was when the apostles preached and taught the resurrection of the Lord Jesus Christ, that they encountered their fiercest opposition.

The importance of our Lord's resurrection is definitely stated by the Apostle Paul when he writes, "Now if Christ be preached that he rose from the dead, how say some among you that there is no resurrection of the dead? But if there be no resurrection of the dead, then is Christ not risen: and if Christ be not risen, then is our preaching vain, and your faith is also vain. Yea, and we are found false witnesses of God; because we have testified of God that he raised up

Christ: whom he raised not up, if so be that the dead rise not. For if the dead rise not, then is not Christ raised: and if Christ be not raised, your faith is vain; and ye are yet in your sins. Then they also which are fallen asleep in Christ are perished. If in this life only we have hope in Christ, we are of all men most miserable. But now is Christ risen from the dead, and become the firstfruits of them that slept" (I Cor. 15: 12-20).

All four of the Gospels record the resurrection of the Lord Jesus Christ. It was foretold by the Old Testament prophets, and also predicted by the Lord Himself. The Epistles explain it.

Biblical Reasons for the Resurrection of the Lord Jesus Christ

1. He Was Raised Again from the Dead Because of Who He Was

He was the Son of God, the Lord of Glory. He was the "Lamb without blemish and without spot." He was "holy, harmless, undefiled, separate from sinners, and made higher than the heavens." Therefore He was not subject to death, it had no claim upon Him. He died because He was made sin, and our sins were laid upon Him. His death accomplished everything necessary for our redemption; therefore death could no longer hold Him.

This is what Peter speaks about on the Day of Pentecost when he says, "Whom God hath raised up, having loosed the pains of death: because it was not possible that he should be holden of it. For David speaketh concerning him, I foresaw the Lord always before my face, for he is on my right hand, that I should not be moved: Therefore did my heart rejoice, and my tongue was glad; moreover also my flesh shall rest in hope: because thou wilt not leave my soul in hell (hades), neither wilt thou suffer thine Holy One to see corruption" (Acts 2:24-27).

Being the Messiah, His resurrection was necessary to vindicate His character from the charges His enemies had filed against Him. He was accused of being an impostor and a blasphemer. His resurrection proved that He was "the Son of God" (Rom. 1:4).

2. He Was Raised Again from the Dead That Prophecy Might Be Fulfilled

God's covenant with David (II Sam. 7:8-17) is concerning the King and the kingdom. It was confirmed with an oath (Psalm 89:3, 4, 35-37), and secured for ever "an house," the Davidic family; a "throne," a symbol of royal authority; a "kingdom," a sphere of rule, and a "king." God said to David, "And when thy days be fulfilled, and thou shalt sleep with thy fathers, I will set thy seed after thee, which shall proceed out of thy bowels, and I will establish his kingdom. He shall build an house for my name, and I will stablish the throne of his kingdom for ever." This refers primarily to Solomon and his kingdom, but its final fulfilment will be realized in and through the Messianic Kingdom.

David had prophesied concerning the resurrection of Christ (Psalm 16:9, 10). Concerning this Peter says, "Therefore being a prophet, and knowing that God had sworn with an oath to him, that of the fruit of his loins, according to the flesh, he would raise up Christ to sit on his throne; he seeing this before spake of the resurrection of Christ, that his soul was not left in hell (hades), neither his flesh did see corruption. This Jesus hath God raised up, whereof we all are witnesses" (Acts 2:30-32).

"Unto you (Israel) first God, having raised up his

Son Jesus, sent him to bless you, in turning away every one of you from his inquities" (Acts 3:26).

3. He Was Raised Again from the Dead Because the Ground of the Sinner's Justification Was Accomplished

God permitted His death, because He required His life as the sacrifice for the sins of the people; He restored it to show that the demands of infinite justice were for ever satisfied. Hence the Scriptures say, "And declared the Son of God with power, according to the spirit of holiness, by the resurrection from the dead" (Rom. 1:4); and that the God of peace brought Him again from the dead through the blood of the everlasting covenant. By this event, God acknowledged Him to be His Son, and gave a solemn assurance that the demands of infinite justice had for ever been satisfied. Paul asks, "Who is he that condemneth? It is Christ that died, yea rather, that is risen again, who is even at the right hand of God, who also maketh intercession for us" (Rom. 8:34).

4. He Was Raised Again from the Dead To Bestow Resurrection Life

He said, "Verily, verily, I say unto you, Except a corn of wheat fall into the ground and die, it abideth alone: but if it die, it bringeth forth much fruit" (John 12:24).

The Apostle Peter in his first epistle declares that the resurrection of our Lord is the means of the new birth; He says, "Blessed be the God and Father of our Lord Jesus Christ, which according to his abundant mercy hath begotten us again unto a lively hope by the resurrection of Jesus Christ from the dead" (I Peter 1:3).

In his second sermon he speaks of our Lord's resurrection in relation to the healing of the lame man. He says, "But ye denied the Holy One and the Just, and desired a murderer to be granted unto you; and killed the Prince of life, whom God hath raised from the dead; whereof we are witnesses. And his name through faith in his name hath made this man strong, whom ye see and know: yea, the faith which is by him hath given him this perfect soundness in the presence of you all" (Acts 3:14-16). The Apostle Paul says, "Wherefore, my brethren, ye also are become dead to the law by the body of Christ; that ye should be married to another, even to him who was raised from the dead, that we should bring forth fruit unto God" (Rom. 7:4).

We are joined to our risen and glorified Lord. It is through this union with Him that we have eternal life. "He is our life." We read, "I am crucified with Christ: nevertheless I live; yet not I, but Christ liveth in me: and the life which I now live in the flesh I live by the faith of the Son of God, who loved me, and gave himself for me" (Gal. 2:20); "For ye are dead, and your life is hid with Christ in God. When Christ, who is our life, shall appear, then shall ye also appear with him in glory" (Col. 3:3, 4).

5. He Was Raised from the Dead To Impart Resurrection Power

The resurrection of the Lord Jesus Christ is God's standard of power today. Paul writes, "The eyes of your understanding (heart) being enlightened; that ye may know what is the hope of his calling, and what the riches of the glory of his inheritance in the saints, and what is the exceeding greatness of his power to usward who believe, according to the working of his mighty power, which he wrought in Christ, when he raised him from the dead, and set him at his own right hand in the heavenly places" (Eph. 1:18-20).

Satan, who is next to God in power, did everything

he possibly could to hinder the coming of our Lord into the world; when Christ came, he did his utmost to destroy Him and to keep Him from going to the cross. When the body of our Lord was placed in the tomb, it was officially sealed and soldiers were placed there to guard it, to make it absolutely sure that Christ would not be raised from the dead; but in spite of all Satan's efforts to the contrary, God raised His Son, our Lord, from the dead.

Today, God exercises this power in our behalf; we are the special objects of His mighty power. It is through this power that we are to live and walk to His glory and honor. It is the power for service and fruit-bearing. "Even so we should walk in the newness of life."

6. He Was Raised from the Dead To Be the Head Over All Things to the Church

"And hath put all things under his feet, and gave him to be the head over all things to the church, which is his body, the fulness of him that filleth all in all" (Eph. 1:22, 23).

Christ is said to be the "head of the corner" (Acts 4:11); the head of the body (Eph. 4:15); the head of every man (I Cor. 11:3) and the head of the church (Eph. 5:25).

He is now the head over all things to the church as His body. In the future He will be the head of the church as the husband is the head of the wife.

7. He Was Raised from the Dead To Be the Firstfruits and the Pattern of the Saints of This Age

We are told, "But now is Christ risen from the dead, and become the firstfruits of them that slept. For since by man came death, by man came also the resurrection of the dead. For as in Adam all die, even so in Christ shall all be made alive. But every man in his own order: Christ the firstfruits; afterward they that are Christ's at his coming" (I Cor. 15:20-23).

Concerning Christ as the pattern, Paul writes, "For our conversation is in heaven; from whence also we look for the Saviour, the Lord Jesus Christ; Who shall change our vile body, that it may be fashioned like unto his glorious body, according to the working whereby he is able even to subdue all things unto himself" (Phil. 3:20, 21). The Apostle John says, "But we know that when he shall appear we shall be like him; for we shall see him as he is" (I John 3:2).

The Lord Jesus Christ was also raised from the dead to be related to the heavenly company of redeemed ones as: the last Adam, the federal head of the new creation (I Cor. 15:45); the Head of the body with its many members (Eph. 5:30; Col. 1:18; 3:15); the True Vine, in whom the saved ones are branches (John 15:1-16); the Foundation and Chief Cornerstone upon whom believers as living stones are "builded together for a habitation of God through the Spirit" (Eph. 2:20-22; I Cor. 3:11); the great High Priest, under whose authority believers as priests minister (Heb. 2:17; I Pet. 2:5, 9); the great Shepherd of the sheep (John 10:1-30; Heb. 13:20); and finally, in the future the Bridegroom of the Church, which is now His body (John 3:29; II Cor. 11:1-3).

The resurrection of the Lord Jesus Christ goes beyond all dispensational bounds and is eternal in its results. It is by the theologians classed as one of the major divine undertakings. It is the proof positive that all that was accomplished by the cross of Christ, to an infinite degree satisfied the eternal demands of divine justice. It is the pledge of our resurrection.

His glorified body is the pattern of what our present bodies will be transformed unto.

"The resurrection of Christ vindicated His character from the aspersions of His enemies. It demonstrated, at the same time, that He had accomplished the work which His Father appointed Him to perform, and had obtained eternal redemption for His people. It gives an assurance to those who believe in Him, of a future triumph over death and the grave. He arose as their representative, and they shall also rise after His example, and through His merits and power." (Dick)

We conclude this chapter with the following words:—"Blessed be the God and Father of our Lord Jesus Christ, which according to his abundant mercy hath begotten us again unto a lively hope by the resurrection of Jesus Christ from the dead, to an inheritance incorruptible, and undefiled, and that fadeth not away, reserved in heaven for you, who are kept by the power of God through faith unto salvation ready to be revealed in the last time" (I Peter 1:3-5).

CHAPTER XII.

THE ASCENSION AND SESSION OF CHRIST

The ascension of our Lord is recorded by two of the Gospel narrators. "So then after the Lord had spoken unto them, he was received up into heaven, and sat on the right hand of God" (Mark 16:19). "And he led them out as far as to Bethany, and he lifted up his hand, and blessed them. And it came to pass while he blessed them, he was parted from them, and carried up into heaven" (Luke 24:50, 51). "And when he had spoken these things, while they beheld, he was taken up; and a cloud received him out of their sight" (Acts 1:9).

A comparison of John 20:17 where we read, "Jesus saith unto her, Touch me not; for I am not yet ascended to my Father: but go to my brethren, and say unto them, I ascend unto my Father, and your Father; and to my God, and your God," with Luke 24:39 where He said to His disciples, "Behold my hands and my feet, that it is I myself: handle me, and see; for a spirit hath not flesh and bones, as ye see me have," reveals two ascensions of our Lord.

On the morning of the resurrection day Christ ascended into heaven, in fulfilment of the wave-sheaf type, the sample and earnest of the mighty harvest that was to follow. So, also, having accomplished the sacrifice for sin, it was necessary for Him to present His blood in heaven. We read, "Neither by the blood of goats and calves, but by his own blood he entered in once into the holy place, having obtained eternal redemption." And, "It was therefore necessary that the patterns of things in the heavens should be purified with these; but the heavenly things themselves with better sacrifices than these" (Heb. 9:12, 23). Read the context; it will do your heart good.

When our Lord ascended the second time—after forty days of post-resurrection ministry—He began His present ministry in behalf of His own. Concerning this we read, "Who being the brightness of his glory, and the express image of his person, and upholding all things by the word of his power, when he had by himself purged our sins, sat down on the right hand of the Majesty on high" (Heb. 1:3); "But this man, after he had offered one sacrifice for sins for ever, sat down on the right hand of God" (Heb. 10:12).

Note that our Lord ascended in His glorified human body and that He now occupies the place of power and honor. He is the man in glory. The man Christ Jesus has left the earth, and entered into that invisible region of the universe where God sits on the throne of His Majesty. To believers, it is a source of consolation to know that He has not laid aside their nature, but retains it in His glorified state and position. They can look up to Him with confidence, in the full assurance of His sympathy, and see, in His exaltation, an earnest of their future glory.

The right hand is the place of honor. It is so reckoned among us, and was so accounted by the Jews. When Solomon's mother came to him, "he sat down on his throne, and caused a seat to be set for the king's mother; and she sat on his right hand. In the position given to our Saviour in heaven, He is invested with great dignity and glory. The words of His intercessory prayer reveal the glory that is His, "And now, O Father, glorify thou me with thine own self with the glory which I had with thee before the world was" (John 17:5).

The right hand is the emblem of power. This is the general idea which is suggested, when hands and arms are attributed to God, because it is with our hands and arms that we exert our strength. The right hand is most commonly used. The sitting of our Saviour at the right hand of God signifies therefore that He is exalted to the place of authority and dominion. "Hereafter," He said to the members of the council, "shall ye see the Son of man sitting on the right hand of power, and coming in the clouds of heaven" (Matt. 26:64).

The fact that when He ascended He was received of His Father is the proof that His earth-ministry was accepted. The fact that He sat down reveals another important truth—that His work was finished. In the earthly tabernacle no place was provided for the high priest to sit down. That was because his work was never finished. When Christ ascended He sat down as the evidence that the work He came into this world to accomplish was once and for all completed.

But note, it was on His Father's throne that He sat down, and not on His own. This proves that He did not set up His kingdom on the earth, when He came the first time, but that He is now "expecting, till his enemies be made his footstool" (Heb. 10:13). Then will the kingdoms of this world become the kingdom of our Lord; and He shall reign for over. The angel told Mary, "He shall be great, and shall be called the Son of the highest: and the Lord God shall give unto him the throne of his Father David: And he shall reign over the house of Jacob for ever; and of his kingdom there shall be no end" (Luke 1:32, 33).

Scripture clearly teaches that He is not now establishing His kingdom-rule in the earth, but rather that He is taking out a people for His name. It is in behalf of this called-out people that our risen and glorified Lord is now ministering.

Our Lord's present ministry in behalf of His own is fourfold.

1. He Is Bestowing Gifts to the Church

"But unto every one of us is given grace according to the measure of the gift of Christ. Wherefore he saith, When he ascended up on high, he led captivity captive, and he gave gifts unto men. And he gave some, apostles; and some, prophets; and some, evangelists; and some, pastors and teachers" (Eph. 4:7, 8, 11).

Note the purpose of these gifts. They are "For the perfecting of the saints, for the work of the ministry, for the edifying of the body of Christ; till we all come in the faith, and of the knowledge of the Son of God, unto a perfect man, unto the measure of the stature of the fulness of Christ" (Eph. 4:12, 13). The true purpose of the ministry is to provide the saints with the equipment necessary for the rendering unto the Lord effectual service. When the saints are so equipped they will no longer be "children, tossed to and fro, and carried about with every wind of doctrine, by the sleight of men, and cunning craftiness, whereby they lie in wait to deceive."

2. He Is Interceding for His Own

Concerning this ministry of our Lord we read, "Who is he that condemneth? Is it Christ, who died, yea rather, who is risen again, who is even at the right hand of God, who also maketh intercession for us?" (Rom. 8:34).

"But this man, because he continueth ever, hath an unchangeable priesthood. Wherefore he is able also to save them to the uttermost that come unto God by him, seeing he ever liveth to make intercession for them" (Heb. 7:24, 25).

Our Lord began this His ministry of intercession, while here on earth. He said to Peter, "Simon, Simon, behold, Satan hath desired to have you, that he might sift you as wheat: but I have prayed for thee, that thy faith fail not: and when thou art converted, strengthen thy brethren" (Luke 22:31, 32).

In His high priestly prayer, He prayed not only for His disciples, but also for all that should believe on Him. He said, "I pray for them: I pray not for the world, but for them which thou hast given me; for they are thine. I pray not that thou shouldest take them out of the world, but that thou shouldest keep them from the evil. Neither pray I for these alone, but for them also which shall believe on me through their word" (John 17:9, 15, 20).

This ministry of our Lord has to do with the weakness, and the helplessness of the saints who are on the earth. He knows their limitations, and the power and the devices of the evil one with whom they have to contend. We read, "For ye were as sheep going astray, but are now returned unto the Shepherd and Bishop of your souls" (I Peter 2:25).

3. Christ Now Appears for His Own in the Presence of God as Advocate

As Christ's ministry of intercession is that the saved ones might not sin, so His advocacy is for the saved one who has sinned. We read, "For Christ is not entered into the holy places made with hands, which are the figures of the true; but into heaven itself, now to appear in the presence of God for us" (Heb. 9:24). An advocate is a lawyer, one who pleads and espouses the cause of another one in the open courts. We need an advocate because we have an accuser—Satan, called "the accuser of the brethren." It is when the child of God sins that Satan appears as the accuser, and it is then that the Lord Jesus Christ advocates for the sinning one. We read, "My little children, these things write I unto you, that ye sin not. And if any man sin, we have an Advocate with the Father, Jesus Christ the righteous: and he is the propitiation for our sins: and not for ours only, but also for the sins of the whole world" (I John 2:1, 2).

He does not excuse our sins, nor does He ask God to be lenient with them. But since He is the propitiation for our sins He pleads His own precious blood shed for them. What He does is infinitely righteous in every respect.

Through our Lord's ministry as Intercessor and Advocate, the child of God is secure for time and eternity.

4. The Lord Jesus Christ Is Now Preparing a Place for His Own

In His farewell message to His own He said, "Let not your heart be troubled: ye believe in God, believe also in me. In my Father's house are many mansions: if it were not so, I would have told you. I go to prepare a place for you. And if I go and prepare a place for you, I will come again, and receive you unto myself; that where I am, there ye may be also" (John 14:1-3). This is the first reference to our Lord's coming for His own—the saints of this dispensation. His own going back to the Father as the glorified man in a very special way enters into this work of His. He is now the man in glory. His going there has opened the way for those who will be glorified with Him.

SECTION FOUR

THE RESULT OF THE ONE ACT OF OBEDIENCE

CHAPTER XIII.

THE NEW CREATION

Through the Apostle Paul, God has given us two great bodies of Truth. In the Epistle to the Romans the Gospel of Grace is unfolded in a systematic way. Romans is The Gospel according to Paul. Concerning this body of truth, he writes, "But I certify you, brethren, that the gospel which was preached of me is not after man. For I neither received it of man, neither was I taught it, but by the revelation of Jesus Christ" (Gal. 1:11, 12).

On this subject we cite Dr. John Brown of Edinburgh. In his exposition of the Epistle to the Galatians he says, "By a direct revelation similar to that which God made known His will to the prophets of old, Paul was made acquainted with that Gospel which he was to preach among the Gentiles. He was not sent to the apostles to be instructed. In the history of his conversion, nothing is said of his receiving instruction from Ananias or the disciples at Antioch. Jesus Christ took him under His own immediate tuition, and made known to him, not only what may be called the abstract part of Christianity, but its leading facts. He received of the Lord an account of the institution of the Lord's Supper. He received of the Lord the Gospel he preached to the Corinthians, 'that Christ died for our sins according to the Scriptures, and that he was buried, and that he rose again the third day according to the

Scriptures.' This statement does not by any means necessarily infer that Paul knew nothing about Jesus Christ but what he learned by revelation. This is certainly in the highest degree improbable. It means that his deep, thorough knowledge of 'the truth as it is in Jesus' was of supernatural origin."

Through the Apostle Paul's ministry our Lord's prophetic statement in John 16:12, 13, where He says, "I have yet many things to say unto you, but ye cannot bear them now. Howbeit when he, the Spirit of truth, is come, he will guide you into all truth: for he shall not speak of himself; but whatsoever he shall hear, that shall he speak: and he will shew you things to come," was in a very special way fulfilled. The other body of truth, of which Paul is the revelator, is concerning "the church, which is his body, the fulness of him that filleth all in all." The church is the New Creation in Christ. The Epistle to the Ephesians is the special revelation concerning the New Creation, but the Apostle Paul speaks about it in his other epistles also. He says, "Therefore if any man be in Christ, he is a new creature (creation): old things have passed away; behold, all things have become new" (II Cor. 5:17); "For in Christ Jesus neither circumcision availeth any thing, nor uncircumcision, but a new creature" (creation) (Gal. 6:15); "For we are his workmanship, created in Christ Jesus unto good works, which God hath before ordained that we should walk in them" (Eph. 2:10); "Having abolished in his flesh the enmity, even the law of commandments, in ordinances; for to make in himself of twain one new man, so making peace" (Eph. 2:15).

Just as the "Gospel of the Kingdom" is the good news concerning God's purpose in the earth, revealing our Lord's relation to the covenant people Israel and the earth, so the "Gospel of the Grace of God" is the good news concerning the finished work of Christ—His death, burial and resurrection. The truth concerning the New Creation reveals the full result of the Gospel of Grace.

When Paul says, "for to make in himself of twain one new man," he does not refer to the saved individual as such, but rather to the whole company of the redeemed ones of this age. The New Creation is the supreme product of the finished work of Christ. It is eternal and infinite in glory.

The Old Creation is Adam, the first man, and every child of Adam in his or her unregenerate state. According to the Scriptures it is Fallen (Rom. 5:12); Sinful (Rom. 5:19, Cf. Gen. 5:3); Evil (Eph. 2:1-3); Depraved (Rom. 3:9-18); Blinded (II Cor. 4:4); Dead in trespasses and sins (Eph. 2:1); Lost (II Cor. 4:3); Energized by Satan (Eph. 2:2); Judged (John 3:18); Condemned (Rom. 8:3); Executed (II Cor. 5:14; Rom. 6:6); Under the sentence of the second death (Rev. 20:14, 15).

The New Creation is Christ, the Second Man, the Last Adam, and every born-again person of the present age. It is the heavenly company, the supreme product of the sacrificial work of Christ.

Concerning Christ in His post-resurrection position we read, "Knowing that Christ being raised from the dead dieth no more; death hath no more dominion over him. For in that he died, he died unto sin once: but in that he liveth, he liveth unto God" (Rom. 6:9, 10).

It is in this, His risen and glorified position, that we as believers are joined to Him. Paul writes, "Wherefore, my brethren, ye also are become dead to the law by the body of Christ; that ye should be married to another, even to him who is raised from the dead, that ye should bring forth fruit unto God" (Rom. 7:4).

As the last Adam, our Lord is the federal head of an entirely new race, a new species. "The first man is of the earth, earthy: the second man is the Lord from heaven. As is the earthy, such are they also that are earthy: and as is the heavenly, such are they also that are heavenly" (I Cor. 15:47, 58).

The New Creation is heavenly in its origin; it is heavenly in its calling; its walk is according to the heavenly standard; and its eternal destiny is heaven.

According to the Word each member of the New Creation has been chosen in Christ (Eph. 1:4); predestinated for adoption as a son (Eph. 1:5); redeemed with the precious blood of Christ (I Peter 1:19); delivered from the Law and its curse (Gal. 4:5; 3:13) by an eternal redemption (Heb. 9:12). He is created in righteousness and true holiness (Eph. 4:24); he is born from above (John 3:3, 6) of the Spirit (John 3:6); and the incorruptible seed (I Peter 1:23); he is reconciled to God (II Cor. 5:19). He is justified freely by His grace (Rom. 3:24; 5:1) and is at peace with Him (Col. 1:20; Rom. 5:1). He is dead to the Law (Rom. 7:4; Gal. 2:19) and passed beyond its reach and jurisdiction (Rom. 6:7; Gal. 3:25); he is free from condemnation (John 5:24; Rom. 8:1, 34). He is complete in Christ (Col. 2:10); accepted in the beloved (Eph. 1:6) and perfected for ever (Heb. 10:14). He is joined to the Lord (I Cor. 6:17) by the Holy Spirit (Gal. 3:27; I Cor. 12:12, 13). He is indwelt by the Spirit who abides for ever (John 14:16, 17) and has been sealed by the Spirit until the day of redemption (Eph. 1:13; 4:30). He is a citizen of heaven (Phil. 3:20) and is already seated with Christ in heavenly places (Eph. 2:6). He is sanctified (I Cor. 1:30); saved (Titus 3:5);

eternally safe and secure (John 10:27-29; Rom. 8:35-39). He is destined for heaven (John 14:1-3; I Thess. 4:13-18). "As he is so are we in this world" (I John 4:17).

Whatever is true concerning the Lord Jesus Christ is also true of every one that is "in Him." This is with reference to the believer's position in Christ. When we read, "For in that he died, he died unto sin once: but in that he liveth, he liveth unto God," we are reminded of the fact that our Lord is forever beyond the reach of death. So, also, has the believer's relation to sin been completely severed. Words could not be plainer than those used by the Apostle Paul when he writes, "Knowing this, that our old man was crucified with him, that the body of sin might be destroyed (rendered powerless), that henceforth we should not serve sin. For he that is dead is freed from sin. Now if we be dead with Christ, we believe that we shall also live with him: Knowing that Christ being raised from the dead dieth no more; death hath no more dominion over him. For in that he died, he died unto sin once: but in that he liveth, he liveth unto God. Likewise reckon ye also yourselves to be dead indeed unto sin, but alive unto God through Jesus Christ our Lord" (Rom. 6:6-11).

These verses reveal our identification with Christ in His death, burial and resurrection. Being identified with Him as our substitute we have set before us our judicial union with Christ. Had we not been of the cross, He never would have been there, because He had no sin or sins to suffer for. Note that Paul says that we died with Christ unto sin. This refers to the sin nature, the old man. Christ's death was not only for sin, but also unto sin. The Apostle Peter tells us that we are dead to sins. Note his words, "Who his own self bare our sins in his own body on the tree, that we, being dead to sins, should live unto righteousness: by whose stripes ye were healed" (I Peter 2:24). When Paul says we are to reckon ourselves dead unto sin, he tells us to accept as true what God says about us. It is not what we think or feel, but what He says.

In each case, the nature of the creation depends upon the act of the head. Paul says, "As is the earthy, such are they also that are earthy; and as is the heavenly, such are they also that are heavenly. And as we have borne the image of the earthy, we shall also bear the image of the heavenly." The full realization of our bearing the image of the heavenly awaits the day, when we who belong to Him, shall be like Him, because we are going to see Him as He is.

When Paul designates the unregenerate as "the sons of disobedience," he is not referring to their personal disobedience, but rather as the natural children of Adam their federal head, in whom all sinned and are therefore the sons of disobedience.

The individual becomes a member of the New Creation when he is created anew in Christ Jesus. This is not accomplished by any works of righteousness, nor by being good, nor by turning over a new leaf as sinners are sometimes urged to do. Neither is it through any religious efforts on the part of the unsaved. Being baptized and becoming a member of a local church organization does not save from sin.

No, it is when the sinner "with the heart believes unto righteousness." He is then joined to the Lord (I Cor. 6:17) by the Holy Spirit (Gal. 3:27; I Cor. 12:12, 13), and is then "blessed with every spiritual blessing in the heavenlies in Christ" (Eph. 1:3). We have already noted some of the many blessings and benefits that constitute the riches of His grace.

And now, note some things concerning the blessings that the believer is blessed with in Christ. It is God the Father who bestows the blessings; they are in Christ the Son, and are not material but spiritual.

Most of them are not experimental. Justification is not something we feel in our emotional nature nor in our nervous system. It is a judicial act of God, and therefore something that takes place in the mind and reckoning of God. Experiences will follow as the result of being declared righteous in Christ. I will never forget the day when I discovered what it meant to be justified. It was years after I was saved. The Lord used an old brother in the Lord to make it known to me. Neither are they progressive; it is not something the believer receives in installments because of any merits of his. Sonship (adoption), another great blessing, is not progressive. The saved one is as much a son the day he is saved as he ever will be in time or eternity. Neither are the blessings in Christ related to human merit, "For by grace are ye saved through faith; and that not of yourselves: it is the gift of God: not of works, lest any man should boast" (Eph. 2:8, 9); "Not by works of righteousness which we had done, but according to his mercy he saved us, by the washing of regeneration, and the renewing of the Holy Ghost" (Titus 3:5); "Being justified freely (without cause) by his grace through the redemption that is in Christ Jesus" (Rom. 3:24); "Who hath saved us, and called us with an holy calling, not according to our works, but according to his purpose, and the grace which was given us in Christ Jesus before the world began, but is now made manifest by the appearing of our Saviour Jesus Christ, who hath abolished death, and hath brought life and immortality to light through the gospel" (II Tim. 1:9, 10).

They are eternal in character, and not something

one possesses one day and not the next. They do not change with the moon, but are fixed facts, and we are called upon to accept them as such, and to rest and rejoice in them. They are known only through the Word.

We have already noted that the New Creation is a new race, a new species. It is the people that the Lord is now taking out for His name. This is accomplished by the preaching of the Gospel of Grace, and the ministry of the Holy Spirit. When the last member has been added to this company of redeemed ones, God's purpose for this age will be completed. The Lord will come for His own. He said, "Let not your heart be troubled: ye believe in God, believe also in me. In my Father's house are many mansions: if it were not so I would have told you. I go to prepare a place for you. And if I go and prepare a place for you, I will come again, and receive you unto myself; that where I am, there ye may be also" (John 14:1-3). The Apostle Paul tells us how this will be accomplished. He writes, "For the Lord himself shall descend from heaven with a shout, with the voice of the archangel, and with the trump of God: and the dead in Christ shall rise first: then we that are alive and remain shall be caught up together with them in the clouds, to meet the Lord in the air: and so shall we ever be with the Lord" (I Thess. 4:16, 17). To the Corinthians he writes, "Behold, I shew you a mystery; we shall not all sleep, but we shall all be changed, in a moment, in the twinkling of an eye, at the last trump: for the trumpet shall sound, and the dead shall be raised incorruptible, and we shall be changed. For this corruptible must put on incorruption, and this mortal must put on immortality" (I Cor. 15:51-53). To the Philippians he writes, "For our conversation is in heaven; from whence also we look for the Saviour, the Lord Jesus Christ: who shall change our vile body, that it may be fashioned like unto his glorious body, according to the working whereby he is able even to subdue all things to himself" (Phil. 3:20, 21). The Apostle John writes, "Beloved, now are we the sons (children) of God, and it doth not yet appear what we shall be: but we know that, when he shall appear, we shall be like him; for we shall see him as he is" (I John 3:2).

The assurance given to us in the Word that our Lord will come for His own has been the hope and comfort of the Lord's people ever since He returned to the Father. It has been one of the greatest incentives in all missionary efforts. Our great missionary leaders have been firm believers in the soon coming of the Lord Jesus Christ. It is also a motive for holiness. "And every one that hath this hope in him purifieth himself, even as he is pure" (I John 3:3).

"Now unto him that is able to keep you from falling, and to present you faultless before the presence of his glory with exceeding joy, to the only wise God our Saviour, be glory and majesty, dominion and power, both now and ever. Amen" (Jude 24, 25).

CHAPTER XIV.

SERVICE AND REWARDS

Through the convicting, regenerating, baptizing, sealing and indwelling ministries of the Holy Spirit a believing sinner becomes a child of God, a member of the body of Christ, the true church, which is now the New Creation in Christ Jesus. When the sinner is saved he becomes a pilgrim and a stranger on the earth. The Apostle Peter says, "Dearly beloved, I beseech you as strangers and pilgrims, abstain from fleshly lusts, which war against the soul" (I Peter 2:11).

From the moment he is born again the saved one is a citizen of heaven. Paul says, "For our conversation (citizenship) is in heaven; from whence also we look for the Saviour, the Lord Jesus Christ" (Phil. 3:20).

The Christian, then, does not belong down here on earth. Yet God leaves him here, and that for a very definite purpose.

If believers would be taken home to be with the Lord when they are saved they would escape many trials, testings, failures and disappointments. Why then does He leave us here on earth? Is it as some say, that we shall through our wilderness journey be fitted for heaven? No! A Christian is no more fitted for heaven after years of devoted service than he was the day he was saved. There is but one thing that can make a lost and guilty sinner fit for heaven, and that is the precious blood of Christ.

Concerning our acceptance with God we read that we are "accepted in the beloved" (Eph. 1:6); "And ye are complete in him" (Col. 2:10); "For by one offering hath he perfected for ever them that are sanctified" (Heb. 10:14). "But of him are ye in Christ Jesus, who of God is made unto us wisdom, and righteousness, and sanctification, and redemption" (I Cor. 1:30).

His true motive in leaving His own here on earth is that they might be His witnesses. We are saved for service. "For we are his workmanship, created in Christ Jesus unto good works, which God hath before ordained that we should walk in them" (Eph. 2:10); "This is a faithful saying, and these things I will that thou affirm constantly, that they which have believed in God might be careful to maintain good works. These things are good and profitable unto men" (Titus 3:8).

It is through the members of the body of Christ, the true church, that the Lord works rather than through man-made organizations. This service the Apostle Paul calls a "labor of love." Our lives as Christians should tell for the Lord, and they will if we as members of His body are rightly adjusted to Him. We are His witnesses in the midst of sin and the evil in the world" (John 15:27). "A faithful witness delivereth souls" (Prov. 14:25).

We are also representatives of His. As ambassadors, we represent the Court of Heaven. A greater honor could be bestowed upon no one.

In His high priestly prayer our Lord said, "As thou hast sent me into the world, even so have I also sent them into the world" (John 17:17).

Concerning His own mission He said, "For I am not come to call the righteous, but sinners to repentance" (Matt. 9:13); "For even the Son of man came not to be ministered unto, but to minister, and to give his life a ransom for many" (Mark 10:45); "For the Son of man is come to seek and to save that which is lost" (Luke 19:10).

The Apostle Paul writes at length regarding our service. He says, "I have planted, Apollos watered; but God gave the increase. So then neither is he that planteth any thing, neither he that watereth; but God that giveth the increase. Now he that planteth and he that watereth are one: and every man shall receive his own reward according to his own labour. For we are labourers together with God: ye are God's husbandry, ye are God's building. According to the grace of God which is given unto me, as a wise masterbuilder, I have laid the foundation, and another buildeth thereon. But let every man take heed how he buildeth thereupon. For other foundation can no man lay than that is laid, which is Jesus Christ. Now if any man build upon this foundation gold, silver, precious stones, wood, hay, stubble; every man's work shall be made manifest: for the day shall declare it, because it shall be revealed by fire; and the fire shall try every man's work of what sort it is. If any man's work abide which he hath built thereupon, he shall receive a reward. If any man's work shall be burned, he shall suffer loss: but he himself shall be saved; yet as by fire" (I Cor. 3:6-15).

In these verses are revealed several important truths in connection with our "labour of love." They speak about service, two classes of building material, judgment and rewards.

Salvation is the gift of God's grace; rewards will

be given according to what we have done after we are saved. "Wherefore we labour, that, whether present or absent, we may be accepted of him. For we must all appear before the judgment seat of Christ; that every one may receive the things done in his body, according to that he hath done, whether it be good or bad" (II Cor. 5:9, 10).

The Judgment Seat of Christ will not be to determine if those who appear there are saved, for only believers will be there. The Scriptures definitely and positively teach that the child of God is past judgment with reference to sin. Our Lord says, "He that believeth on him is not condemned: but he that believeth not is condemned already, because he hath not believed in the name of the only begotten Son of God" (John 3:18); "Verily, verily, I say unto you, He that heareth my words, and believeth on him that sent me, hath everlasting life, and shall not come into condemnation; but is passed from death unto life" (John 5:24); "All that the Father hath given me shall come to me; and him that cometh unto me I will in no wise cast out" (John 6:37). Paul writes, "For if we would judge ourselves we should not be judged. But when we are judged, we are chastened of the Lord, that we should not be condemned with the world" (I Cor. 11: 31, 32).

We must distinguish between the guilt and the defilement of sin. When Paul writes, "Blessed is the man to whom the Lord will not impute sin" (Rom. 4:8), he is referring to the guilt of sin. The context clearly reveals in a most unmistakable way that he is speaking about the one that God has justified, declared righteous in Christ. To the justified one sin is not imputed as guilt. In another place he says, "Who shall lay any thing to the charge of God's elect? It is God that justifieth." No, for then the justified one would have to be brought into court again and convicted anew, which is a thing that God will not do with a child of His. He will chasten him, and that even unto physical death.

However, the result of sin in the life of the believer is most serious. The Holy Spirit is grieved, and so His indwelling ministry is hindered. Fellowship is broken; the contact for power and service destroyed; prayer is hindered, and the joy of salvation is lost. The sinning one is restored when he confesses his sin. This is self-judgment. If he refuses to judge himself God will judge him, but never condemn him with the world. Until the sinning one has judged himself, he is as a dislocated limb in the body.

It is before the Judgment Seat of Christ that "every man's work shall be made manifest," and "the fire shall try every man's work of what sort it is." Fire is a symbol of judgment, and is so used in the Scriptures. When John the Baptist said about Christ, "He shall baptize you with the Holy Ghost, and with fire," he referred to two different classes. The chaff, which represents the unbelievers, will be burned with unquenchable fire.

The purpose of this judgment will be to determine the rewards of the Lord's servants. At the Great White Throne there will be degrees of punishment for the wicked, because they will be judged according to their works. This principle will also apply to the judgment of the believer's works at the Judgment Seat of Christ; there will be degrees of rewards.

The Apostle John says, "Look to yourselves, that we lose not those things which we have wrought, but that we receive a full reward" (II John 1:8).

Some one asks, "How may I know if I am building

with the kind of material that will bring me a reward?"

The answer is to be found in the Word of God. Turn again to First Corinthians, where the Apostle Paul says, "For if I do this thing willingly, I have a reward" (I Cor. 9:17).

These words reveal that it is the motive in our service that determines whether we will receive a reward or not. What we do willingly is a "labour of love" and such our service for the Lord should always be.

All true Christian service is committed to a divinely appointed and qualified people. In the Old Testament the service was committed to the priesthood. Israel had a priesthood. The Church is a priesthood. The priests were appointed to render service toward man. Not until we have first rendered our service toward God are we qualified to render any service toward man.

Our service toward God is threefold. The first is the service of sacrifice, which itself is threefold: (1) the sacrifice of self,—"I beseech you therefore, brethren, by the mercies of God, that ye present your bodies a living sacrifice, holy, acceptable unto God, which is your reasonable (logical) service" (Rom. 12:1); (2) the sacrifice of praise,—"By him therefore let us offer the sacrifice of praise to God continually, that is, the fruit of our lips giving thanks to his name" (Heb. 13:15); (3) the sacrifice of substance,—"But to do good and to communicate forget not: for with such sacrifices God is well pleased" (Heb. 13:16).

The second Christian service is that of worship which is again of self, of praise and of substance? It is true devotion to Christ, and is in and through Him alone.

TWO MEN, TWO ACTS, TWO RESULTS

The third is the service of intercession (I Tim. 2:1). This is one of the believer's greatest privileges, and a most important and effectual service toward God.

Every true believer is constituted a priest. The ministry of the Old Testament priest was threefold. It was to offer sacrifices for the people, to go within the veil and make intercession, and to come forth and bless the people.

Before he could enter upon his ministry as priest he had to be consecrated. Regarding this we are told, "And Moses brought Aaron and his sons, and washed them with water. And he brought the other ram, the ram of consecration: and Aaron and his sons laid their hands upon the head of the ram. And he slew it; and Moses took of the blood of it, and put it upon the tip of Aaron's right ear, and upon the thumb of his right hand, and upon the great toe of his right foot. And he brought Aaron's sons, and Moses put of the blood upon their right ear, and upon the thumbs of their right hands, and upon the great toes of their right feet: and Moses sprinkled the blood upon the altar round about. And Moses took of the anointing oil, and of the blood that was upon the altar, and sprinkled it upon Aaron, and upon his garments, and upon his sons, and upon his sons' garments with him, and sanctified Aaron, and his garments, and his sons, and his sons' garments with him" (Lev. 8:6, 22-24, 30).

Note that the anointing oil was poured upon Aaron (Lev. 8:12) before the blood was applied. Aaron was a type of Christ as the Sinless One who required no preparation for receiving the anointing oil, the symbol of the Holy Spirit.

The initial washing was once for all. But after that, it was necessary for the priests to wash their hands and their feet before they entered the tabernacle to minister. Defilement disqualified the priests for service. Cleansing was absolutely necessary. So today, defilement disqualifies the believer-priest for service. The blood of Christ is the means of perpetual cleansing. The need is clearly set forth by our Lord when He washed His disciples' feet (John 13:1-11).

When we as priests have been consecrated (consecration is a work of God and not of man); when we have offered our sacrifices, and have been within the veil and made intercession, we are qualified to go forth and be a blessing to others.

Our service toward our fellow man is primarily the exercise of a gift. "Now there are diversities of gifts, but the same Spirit. And there are differences of administrations, but the same Lord. And there are diversities of operations, but it is the same God which worketh all in all, but the manifestation of the Spirit is given to every man to profit withal" (I Cor. 12:4-7).

A gift is the manifestation of the Spirit. He may recognize the native ability of the individual, but he is most certainly not dependent upon it. It is when the child of God is rightly adjusted to the Lord and to the Holy Spirit, that the Spirit will manifest Himself in some gift. The exercise of that gift is true Christian service toward man. And it is when such a gift is willingly exercised that we have a reward.

The Apostle Paul also discloses the method of his ministry. Summing it up, he says, "For though I be free from all men, yet have I made myself servant unto all, that I might gain the more. To the weak became I as weak, that I might gain the weak: I am made all things to all men, that I might by all means save some. And every man that striveth for the mastery is temperate in all things. Now they do it to obtain a corruptible crown, but we an incorruptible" (I Cor. 9:19, 22, 25).

Here Paul likens the believer's service to a race. He likewise reminds us of the need of being temperate in all things. He seems to have been fond of agonistic metaphors borrowed from the stadium and the arena. He tells how one may be qualified to run in the race, adding "SO run, that ye may obtain."

Then the Apostle goes on to tell us how he was running in the race, and how he was endeavoring to keep fit. He says, "But I keep under my body, and bring it into subjection: lest that by any means, when I have preached to others, I myself should be a castaway" (I Cor. 9:27).

When Paul says, "I myself should be a castaway," he is not concerned with salvation but rewards. No, Paul could say, "I know whom I have believed, and am persuaded that he is able to keep that which I have committed (my deposit) unto him against that day" (II Tim. 1:12). Happy are they who can share this assurance with the great apostle to the Gentiles!

Paul says, "Know ye not that they which run in a race run all, but one receiveth the prize?"

In another verse he asks, "What is my reward then?" Whatever it will be, the New Testament writers use the word "crown" when speaking about the reward of the believer. They disclose five crowns, and for what they are given.

The Crown of Life is given to those who endure temptations and trials, and that love Him. We read, "Blessed is the man that endureth temptation: for when he is tried, he shall receive the crown of life, which the Lord hath promised to them that love him" (James 1:12); "Fear none of those things which thou shalt suffer: behold the devil shall cast some of you in prison, that ye may be tried; and ye shall have tribulation ten days: be thou faithful unto death, and I will give thee the crown of life" (Rev. 2:10).

The Incorruptible Crown will be given to those who win in the race. "So run, that ye may obtain." "Wherefore seeing we also are compassed about with so great a cloud of witnesses, let us lay aside every weight, and the sin which doth so easily beset us, and let us run with patience the race that is set before us, looking unto Jesus the author and finisher of our faith; who for the joy that was set before him endured the cross, despising the shame, and is set down at the right hand of the throne of God" (Heb. 12:1, 2).

The Unfading Crown of Glory. "And when the chief Shepherd shall appear, ye shall receive the crown of glory that fadeth not away" (I Peter 5:4). These words Peter addresses to the elders admonishing them to so work that they will receive the crown of glory that fadeth not away. This crown will be given to all who have helped shepherd the flock of God.

The Crown of Righteousness will be given to "all those who have loved his appearing." We quote the whole paragraph in order that we may get the true meaning of the apostle's words concerning this crown. The advocates of a partial rapture theory have made use of this part of the Word to prove their position. Paul says, "For I am now ready to be offered, and the time of my departure is at hand. I have fought a good fight, I have finished my course, I have kept the faith: henceforth there is laid up for me a crown of righteousness, which the Lord, the righteous judge, shall give me at that day: and not to me only, but unto all them that have loved his appearing" (II Tim. 4:6-8).

Paul could look back upon a very strenuous

career. His firm belief in the imminent return of the Lord had encouraged him all along the way. Now he was ready for his home going; he therefore looked to the future and to what he as a servant of the Lord was going to receive. But note that he says, "at that day"—the day that all believers will appear before the Judgment Seat of Christ. Not until then will the Apostle Paul nor any other servant of the Lord receive his reward; not until then will all the returns of his labor be in.

The Crown of Rejoicing is the crown that will be the portion of the soul-winner.

To the Thessalonians Paul writes, "For what is our hope, or joy, or crown of rejoicing? Are not even ye in the presence of our Lord Jesus Christ at his coming? For ye are our glory and joy" (I Thess. 2:19, 20), and to the Philippians, "Therefore, my brethren dearly beloved and longed for, my joy and crown, so stand fast in the Lord, my dearly beloved" (Phil. 4:1).

Paul had spent but very little time in Philippi and in Thessalonica. But in those places as well as in the other places he labored, souls had been won for the Lord. Whatsoever was accomplished through the labors of this faithful servant of the Lord, he gave all the glory to God. He says, "So then neither is he that planteth any thing, neither he that watereth; but God that giveth the increase" (I Cor. 3:7).

We should strive for a full reward, because the glory will be our Lord's. "And when those beasts give glory and honour and thanks to him that sat on the throne, who liveth for ever and ever, the four and twenty elders fall down before him that sat on the throne, and worship him that liveth for ever and ever, and cast their crowns before the throne, saying, Thou art worthy, O Lord, to receive glory and honour and power: for thou hast created all things, and for thy pleasure they are and were created" (Rev. 4:9-11).

He alone is worthy of this glory, honor and praise. He it was that brought us up also out of an horrible pit, out of the miry clay, and set our feet upon a rock, and established our goings. It is the Lord who originates, inaugurates, advances and consummates the whole of our salvation.

He saves us, provides us with a working capital and gives us a reward if we have built with the right kind of material.

The New Creation is heavenly in its calling; its rule of life is Grace, the heavenly standard. Its conflict is in the heavenlies, "For we wrestle not against flesh and blood, but against principalities, against powers, against the rulers of the darkness of this world, against spiritual wickedness in high places" (Eph. 6:12).

The New Creation in Christ Jesus is destined for heaven, the abode of "God the judge of all," "Jesus Christ the Mediator of the New Covenant," "an innumerable company of angels," "the spirits of just men made perfect," "and the general assembly and the church of the first born."

And now, my dear reader, which one of the two creations do you belong to? Unless you have put your trust in Christ and accepted Him as your personal Saviour, yea, as the sacrifice that God provided for your sin and your sins, you are still a part of the old creation, absolutely lost and bound for the eternal abode of the lost.

If you have ceased from your own works and with the heart believed unto righteousness you are a member of the New Creation, perfectly saved and safe in Christ for time and eternity. Which is it? There is no intermediate ground.

"Now the God of peace, that brought again from the dead our Lord Jesus, that great shepherd of the sheep, through the blood of the everlasting covenant, make you perfect in every good work to do his will, working in you that which is well pleasing in his sight, through Jesus Christ; to whom be glory for ever and ever. Amen."

www.ingramcontent.com/pod-product-compliance
Lightning Source LLC
Chambersburg PA
CBHW051109160426
43193CB00010B/1374